Less is More

Harriet Walker

Less is More
Minimalism in Fashion

MERRELL
LONDON · NEW YORK

Introduction

Minimalism is a source
of constant inspiration to
fashion designers wishing
to reinvent the codes of
womenswear. Nude body
by Fogal, silk trousers by
Yves Saint Laurent.

Any history of fashion in the twentieth century is a history of minimalism. There are few schools of thought, philosophy or design that have been so consistently reused and revisited across the discipline, and by such a cross-section of influential designers, whether creatively, commercially or conceptually. Some of the finest practitioners and biggest names in modern fashion, from Coco Chanel and Cristóbal Balenciaga via Rei Kawakubo and Martin Margiela to Hussein Chalayan, have made it their source and its tenets their modes of expression.

Minimalism might be considered a starting point, a blank sheet or *tabula rasa* from which all originates and to which, in times of excess and distress, designers return to renew themselves. Just as the art of line drawing is a prerequisite for certain types of painting, so minimalism has to do with an awareness of the fundamentals, the building blocks of fashion design. But if minimalism is in essence about first principles, there is nevertheless a story to be told about its own evolution through the numerous periodic re-emergences whereby it makes its influence felt in successive socio-historical contexts.

As a concept, minimalism is not easy to delineate. On the one hand, it is defined rather nebulously by what it is not; on the other, it can seem a stringent and restrictive aesthetic to work to or live by. The term officially came into being in the 1960s, when a group of artists in New York rejected the traditional representations in painting and sculpture and chose to pursue a new mode that owed as little as possible to the physical existence of an object. The artist Donald Judd, working throughout the 1960s, became known for his use of industrial materials to create abstract works that defied immediate categorization and explored purity of shape and colour. His *Untitled* (1968; overleaf) features a series of anodized aluminium and acrylic tray-like layers stacked on top of one another, without touching, and attached to a wall. Judd described his work as 'the simple expression of complex thought', and this fairly sums up the aesthetic as it exists within fashion, too, its aim from its inception to create pragmatic and functional but technically sophisticated womenswear.

That birth came well before minimalism had been accommodated to the labels of the 1960s and beyond, and is the starting point of this book. The simplification of dress that occurred in the early decades of the twentieth century is undeniably minimalist *avant la lettre*, but does it count as such without a defining watchword having yet been invented? Of course. Artists and architects were working under the precepts of 'modernism' well before the minimalist movement, and the sort of sartorial reduction championed by such designers as Chanel can just as easily be termed modernist as called minimalist, but the main function of her work was to strip away that which was unnecessary and which impaired function. Just as modernist authors were abandoning the rhetorical curlicues of Victorian and Edwardian novelists, and the 1920s Bauhaus movement in architecture worked with a clear aim of practicality and pragmatism, early fashion designers sought to reassess the values inherent in womenswear at the time. Modernity at this point necessitated a paring down and a clarifying of line, silhouette and content.

Descriptions and definitions of minimalism tend to be abstract, which is why this book endeavours to provide for each of the designers discussed concrete examples of clothing that illustrate why the pieces and their creators can be classed as minimalist or minimalists. Broadly speaking, the defining aspect is a lack of any embellishment. A Balenciaga gown covered in appliqué flowers is not obviously minimalist, but the same designer's architectural amphora-line dresses, with their clean lines and lack of surface adornment, are. Decoration and minimalism are not mutually exclusive, but any embellishment should come by way of structure and construction. In a garment, there should be no elements extraneous to construction; every part should

Introduction

DONALD JUDD

Untitled, 1968
The artist Donald Judd
describes his minimalist
pieces as 'the simple
expression of complex
thought'.

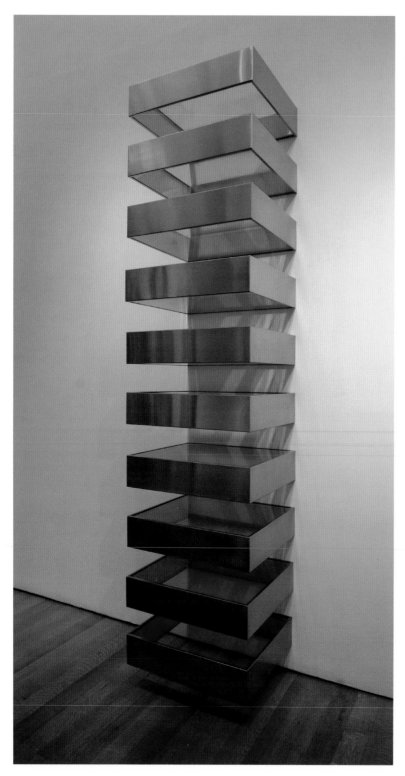

be an essential panel or plane. Minimalism eschews the superfluous and superficial.

The traditional view of the fashionable minimalist is a rather severe-looking intellectual wearing a shapeless black sack. This might not be too far from the mark; minimalism has a reputation, an archetype even, for being challenging, deliberately academic and rarefied, a fact backed up by the didacticism that has come with some of its incarnations. Given that the look has anticipated some of the biggest overhauls of fashion sense, taste and fashionability in the twentieth century, it holds a certain attraction for absolutists, designers and consumers alike. Chanel was one such evangelical, as were Pierre Cardin and André Courrèges, with their fashionable proselytizing on all things streamlined and futuristic. Minimalism has often seemed an exclusive club, for the intellectuals and the avant-garde only, but this book seeks to explain how the aesthetic is fundamental to a much broader social spectrum, and to highlight the ways in which it has been adapted to fit into differing eras and conflicting zeitgeists. The vagaries of form and silhouette – especially the interplay between garment and body – are crucial to the progression and mutation of minimalism; body-consciousness has been as important an aspect of the aesthetic and its development as shapelessness. So have colour and structure: where designers have fused architectural construction with minimalism, that, too, is in reference to creating a simplified line at its most extreme and most graphic. The simplest-looking garment holds within it countless complexities.

If the instinct towards minimalism is, then, intrinsic to the modern mindset, that instinct took time to find its expression. Reduction has been a reflex throughout twentieth-century fashion, a reactionary aesthetic impulse to create clothes and design more suited to their contexts. When Chanel opened her first clothing boutiques in the French seaside towns of Deauville and Biarritz, she was selling simple jersey and cotton sportswear to a public more used to sitting on the beach in corsets and petticoats, or suits and stovepipe hats. Early minimalism in fashion was arguably one with that wider change in sensibilities that Virginia Woolf dated, with magnificent disregard for the First World War, to 'on or about December 1910', in her essay 'Mr. Bennett and Mrs. Brown' of 1924.

In the creation of functional clothes in which women could move, live, travel and – crucially – work, minimalism is undoubtedly one of the most important tropes of modern fashion. From getting the vote to getting jobs, from winning recognition in the workplace to 'having it all', the story of the ascendance of the modern woman is mirrored by the rise and fall of popular minimalism as a fashionable aesthetic; it could be said that her wardrobe becomes simpler to enable her better to deal with the complexities of her lifestyle and its multiplying demands. Interestingly, setbacks on that road to a parity of gender opportunities have also been key to the development of minimalism: the backlashes against feminism in the 1950s and 1980s saw a return in fashion to a hyper-feminine look, by Christian Dior and by the likes of Thierry Mugler and Christian Lacroix respectively, but such regressions were inevitably overturned by a new wave of avant-garde designers working in a reductivist mode. In all its many guises, minimalism is a marker of social progress.

The paring-down of clothing has effectively been one of the most egalitarian popular movements in modern design. It has manifested itself, somewhat paradoxically, at the opposing extremes of economic cycles. At the height of a boom, the culture of excess begets a reaction and a return to simplicity; when boom turns to bust, minimalism has provided a means of reconstructing consumer mores and reinvigorating fashion. After both world wars, designers – as well as governments and the populace – turned to minimalism as a lifestyle choice. Whether termed utility or austerity, .

simplification in matters of fashion and dress is fundamental to modern existence; any record of latter-day consumerism is a story of the ebb and flow in popularity of minimalism in fashion. In this respect, minimalism or reductivism provides the weft and weave of modern sociocultural fabric, with its linear existence at the heart of modernism and its cyclical reappearance as an expression of fashion.

Minimalism is also a consistent indicator of market forces and technological advances. Before the days of mass production, the couture tradition of artisanal craftsmanship was a by-product of the way the fashion industry worked, albeit servicing a very high-level clientele. After the introduction of industrial-scale retail and mass-market clothing in the early 1900s, couture became increasingly difficult to justify, and it became clear that its remit did not necessarily encompass the progressive field of minimalism. With mass production came mass simplification. The American sportswear designers were the first and the best-versed in designing clothes to suit production methods, and the way to do that was to simplify patterns and distil garments to their essence. Minimalism at this point became an exciting means of recasting what had gone before, of remaking it according to standardized modes of working and living. This observation acquires telling force when we consider the work of Kawakubo and Margiela, who altered the very machines that had made mass minimalism possible to create 'la mode destroy': ripped and recalibrated pieces, which were produced on machines with the aim of making them pristinely and systematically pulled apart.

It is indeed a mark of the fertility and diversity of minimalism that it accommodates such antitheses. Its practical origins may at one time have marked it out as a levelling concept in fashion. That is doubtless still true, but modern minimalism, especially that of the early twenty-first-century revival, has been concerned with the fusion of its heritage of utility and austerity with its tendency towards absolutism. The focus of this absolutism in recent seasons has been a need for quality and a litotic emphasis on luxury. Thus modern minimalism has managed to straddle the seemingly polar opposite tropes of reduction and excess by creating plain, sober garments in the richest, most luxurious fabrics available. This sense of luxe now has a place in what we term minimalism. The accusations of intellectualism, pretension and high-mindedness that often accompany the aesthetic were founded originally on its divergence from the mainstream and the distinctly 'anti-fashion' stance of its followers. Modern minimalism, however, becomes the target for such objections because of its price – because, in essence, it has been subsumed into the high-fashion machine. It is perhaps a pointer to the protean nature of minimalism that it is able to veer from an egalitarian mode to a profoundly hierarchical one.

'Minimalism is less brainy today, more hedonistic and instinctive', says Jil Sander.[1] The aesthetic is singular in its headcount of visionary female designers, and if Chanel is its mother, Sander is definitely its aunt or big sister. As discussed, minimalism in fashion provides a way of working and dressing that makes the feminine existence easier. Chanel, Claire McCardell, Donna Karan and Sander all vocalized as much, but it is interesting to note that the clutch of designers currently spearheading the minimalist movement – Phoebe Philo at Céline, Stella McCartney and Hannah MacGibbon for Chloé – are thirty-something women who became known for a certain girlishness in their earlier designs, and who grew up in the women's liberation era of the 1970s. 'Hence the focus on believable daywear,' wrote Penny Martin in 2010, 'the sturdy fabrics and sympathetic cutting and, above all, the charmingly frumpy palette of camel, khaki and beige.'[2] It is further proof of the intricacies of minimalism that its current revival can encapsulate 'charmingly frumpy' as well as the futuristic vision of such designers as Matthew Ames and the casual, sporty tailoring of such newcomers as Damir Doma and Alexander Wang.

The codification of the concept of course requires a specific lexicon. The term 'minimalism' in this book shall refer to that school of design that considers sartorial simplification its goal; it is used as such with no reference to the Minimalism movement in art, which, although by definition similar, holds slightly different tenets at its heart. Purism is also a recurring concept, but this is a rather more context-based interpretation of the minimalist movement within fashion, coined in the late 1980s with reference to the work of such designers as Sander and Calvin Klein. Many designers prefer the term 'pure' to 'minimal' because they feel that minimalism implies a type of emptiness or barrenness, but, as stated, minimalism is a classification only, with no implication of value judgement. It is helpful for the reader because of the sense of agency within it, the act of minimizing one guise into a new and more easily handled form.

'Reductivism' derives from a 1950s art movement, which concentrated on the extreme simplification of form and colour; the meaning is similar in the present context, but emphasizes more the sense of a stripping away and distillation that the term 'minimalism' does not. One can create minimalist clothing without being a reductivist. Likewise, the notion of 'paring down' is integral to the practice and progression of minimalism, and is a useful phrase for the action it implies: a sort of planing down of surface layers, a whittling to find a core or essence.

This active quest for reduction is explored by many designers in their catwalk shows, where theatricality can help to convey the concept that is woven into the clothes. Chalayan's shows are notoriously groundbreaking and visionary in their performative aspects, but Kawakubo's early Comme des Garçons shows also tackled head-on the bourgeois nature of mainstream fashion and the status of women within it. Many found tasteless her *défilés* of pale models wearing no

Such young designers as
Matthew Ames (right) and
Damir Doma (right, bottom)
are part of the latest
generation to choose
minimalism as a means
of expressing the
contemporary mindset.

Introduction

Hooded models at the Autumn/Winter 2005–06 Maison Martin Margiela show (right) and graphic hair and make-up at the Autumn/Winter 2009–10 Yohji Yamamoto show (right, bottom) highlight the performative aspects of minimalism in fashion.

make-up but for vivid purple 'bruises', black eyes and muddied faces, dressed in her signature swagged, faded, ripped and dishevelled pieces. Kawakubo explored the importance of negation in fashion; minimalism was inherent in her very presentation. She would also, when visiting buyers on selling appointments, take a catalogue of her collections on models with her, so formless and unfathomable were the garments on their hangers.

Margiela took to covering his models' faces, whether with his trademark 'incognito' sunglasses or with a square of flesh-toned nylon tied behind the head; such images invoke a near-Beckettian absence as an essential in the minimalist *mise en scène*. There should be nothing to detract from the clothes themselves; or, conversely and dependent on viewpoint, the clothes should not detract from the elemental physicality of the body they clothe. They must also exist in a non-referential, timeless sphere – an aspect that has acquired much economic importance of late in a climate in which consumers are loath to spend money on time-bound ephemera.

A dialogue between time and timelessness runs through the progression of the minimalist aesthetic: witness minimalism's first focus on the futuristic and its current nod towards nostalgia. In striving to be non-referential, many minimalist designers take clothing beyond the seasonal cycle of autumn and spring trends and place them in a more historicized context: such designers as Yohji Yamamoto and Issey Miyake often reference traditional Japanese workwear in their collections, for example. Minimalism is not concerned with progress for the sake of it; rather, it looks to encapsulate the best, most artistic, pragmatic and functional aspects of what has come before, and it is this melding of past success with a thoroughly modern outlook that has seen it transcend the realm of 'fast fashion' or throwaway, 'of the moment' pieces. This also means that minimalist tendencies to refresh and reinvigorate can be tempered by an acknowledgement of

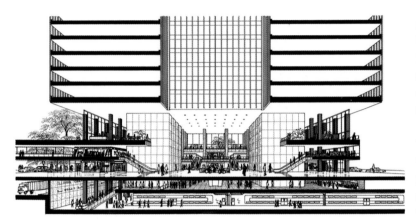

MIES VAN DER ROHE

The Illinois Center, Chicago (1970), by the architect Ludwig Mies van der Rohe, is a prime example of the everyday functionality of minimalist design.

the weight of fashion history and a historicist approach to design.

Such historicism finds an influence in Japanese culture, which, through Shintoism and the practice of Zen, preaches an easy harmony between archetypes and prototypes, between the traditional and the modern. The kimono has been and is still an important reference point for many designers working in a reductivist mode, from Paul Poiret to Gareth Pugh, given its symbolism and its nature as a timeless garment from which anything extraneous has been eliminated. Such a starting point provides another blank canvas, the means for a synthesis and abstraction of clothing that give form to something entirely new. The Japanese philosophy of *wabi-sabi*, an acceptance of transience that informs much of the contrived rusticism in Japanese culture, is also inherent to minimalism in fashion and the aim of producing functional and durable clothing.

During the 1920s and 1930s the Westernization of these ideologies resulted in the Bauhaus and De Stijl movements in art and Brutalism in architecture, all of which focused on the reduction of objects to their essential functions and introduced the inherited notions of minimalist pieces taking angular, graphic forms. Musicians, too – Michael Nyman, Philip Glass and John Tavener, for example – have taken minimalism as a method of composing. The designs and works of Piet Mondrian (which would be overtly

referenced by none other than Yves Saint Laurent), in particular, as well as those of artist Donald Judd and architects Walter Gropius and Ludwig Mies van der Rohe, facilitated the acceptance of minimalism as a mainstream creative avenue.

The title of this book is a quotation from Mies: 'less is more' is the aphorism under which he worked throughout his life. His buildings are the perfect synthesis of the minimalist idiom, of form and function, of the aesthetic and the pragmatic, with each element working in several guises: a floor serves as a radiator, a window as a wall. It is this fusion that underpins minimalism in fashion; the timeless elegance of these garments is belied by the complexities of their conception and construction. This book seeks to offer an appreciation of those designers who have wrung more from less, and in so doing to demonstrate that minimalism is, and always has been, at the heart of modern fashion.

Notes
1 Email from Jil Sander, May 2010.
2 Penny Martin, 'Phoebe Philo Designs the Clothes Women Actually Want to Wear', *The Gentlewoman* 1 (Spring/ Summer 2010), p. 51.

Less is ... New

The Simplification of Womenswear in the Modern Era, 1906–43

'My dear, who are you in mourning for?' designer Paul Poiret is said to have asked Gabrielle 'Coco' Chanel of her modish all-black ensembles when they met in the early 1920s.

'For you, dear Monsieur!' came the response.[1]

Apocryphal though it may be, this exchange highlights the most important trope in fashion at that time: the shift from nineteenth-century sensibilities to those more in line with the twentieth century. Similar alignments had taken place in the art world, with the onset of Modernism and the Art Deco movement, and in literature, with Virginia Woolf and James Joyce taking over from the Edwardians Arnold Bennett and John Galsworthy.

Poiret (1879–1944) was a reformist designer himself, a modernizer and taste-maker in the early years of the century, whose sack dresses and Directoire-line pieces, kimono jackets and tunics had liberated women from the rigid corsetry of an earlier age. At the turn of the century, women were wearing S-bend corsets (known as *la Gache-Sarraute* after their inventor, Inès Gache-Sarraute), which emphasized the bust and the bustle. 'I waged war upon it', declares Poiret in his memoirs. 'It divided the wearer into two distinct sections: on one side, there was the bust and bosom, on the other, the whole behindward aspect, so that the lady looked as though she were hauling a trailer.'[2]

Several attempts had already been made to loosen women's dresses, so to speak, at the close of the previous century. Again, these had been purely aesthetically driven, rather than the result of any concern for the female innards that were being crushed under so many bands of whalebone and steel. Those involved in the Aesthetic movement of the 1880s, among whom were painters Albert Moore and Edward Burne-Jones, held that dress should be freed from convention, simplified and made from classical models. In particular, they did not hold with the hyperbolic prudishness and moralizing of the day, and

believed that women should be able to move freely in their clothes. The first exhibition of the National Health Society in 1882 included dresses made from so-called classical patterns, but which owed rather more to contemporaneous design, and were merely embellished with Graeco-Roman flourishes.

Indeed, some of the first examples of minimalist clothing came not from fashion designers per se, but from neoclassical artists, who began dressing their models in nostalgic, free-flowing Grecian chitons. Dancers, too, such as Isadora Duncan, took up the style, and it was as ballet costumes that the beau monde first became familiar with the gauzy, draped lines of Spanish-born Venetian designer Mariano Fortuny y Madrazo (1871–1949).

Fortuny took as his inspiration ancient statues and hieroglyphs, and was known first for the 'Knossos' scarves he created as costumes for a ballet in 1906. Printed with Cycladic patterns, these rectangular pieces of fabric could be tied in several ways – about the head and shoulders, around the neck, over clothes and pinned at the bust or waist – and represented a new freedom of dress. They quickly became popular among the fashionable set.

The scarves themselves were not minimalist per se, being graphic and colourful (as well as intended for wearing over rather more flamboyant pre-existing outfits), but they were an important first step in terms of changing attitudes to the versatility of womenswear, the alliance of fabric and form, and the practical reuse of clothes, as well as ideas of mixing separates and techniques of layering.

After this first success, Fortuny diversified into other pieces, and by the early 1920s his 'Delphos' dress had become an international phenomenon, the 'It bag' of its day, coveted by every lady of fashion. The dress itself was notable for its absolute simplicity: two panels of thin silk were cut out flat, in the manner of a kimono, and fashioned into a chiton by being joined at the

1905: A woman in typical Edwardian dress. A chemise-style top accentuates the bust; a full skirt drapes from the narrow waist; and decoration comes by way of frills, lace panelling, swagging and pleating, as well as bows, tucks and ruffles. The wide-brimmed hat was essential for any formal outing.

adjustable drawstring was free-flowing, could be worn belted or not, and was a departure from the trussing and froth of contemporary womenswear. Scandalously, there was no need for undergarments or the usual rigours of dressing. The dresses were also very plain (although they came in a spectrum of jewel colours and pastel brights), with no prints or embellishments, as the ideology behind them was one of naturalism, practicality and ease. The aesthetic was meant to be instinctively nonchalant, like the libation-bearers of a Burne-Jones painting, for instance, with none of the artifice usually associated with the belle époque. However, there is no sense of Fortuny as a modernizer: he steadfastly rejected the hard lines and angles of Art Deco, preferring the softer romanticism and nostalgia of the Aesthetes. He was no couturier in the official sense, either (although Cristóbal Balenciaga later dubbed him Spain's greatest), for once he had found his ideal garment he did not develop or deviate from it, working only to improve the technical aspects of the process. The argument for simplicity, in Fortuny's case, was that his timeless dress would not be subject to the whims of fashion.

This, of course, makes Fortuny more modern than he could ever have realized: in this respect, he was the first 'anti-fashion' fashion designer. A common, even overriding, property of the minimalist designer is the refining and condensing process to find an absolute essence of expression in clothing, untempered by zeitgeist or commercial trends. Fortuny's Delphos dress – named after an ancient statuette, the 'Delphic Charioteer', which wears an unadorned, bronze-clasped chiton – is the quintessence of the designer's own vision of femininity. In concentrating on the one piece that truly expressed his ideology, Fortuny foreshadowed such designers as Zoran and Donna Karan, who work each season on the signature pieces that best embody their sartorial manifesto. Fortuny created capes, boleros and evening jackets to be worn over the Delphos, but

shoulders. It was tightly pleated in a process Fortuny himself developed and patented in 1909. The wet silk was tightly folded and left to dry on a system of heated porcelain tubes; as the water evaporated, the silk remained permanently warped into the folded shape. Buyers were advised to keep the dresses wound and knotted in storage or when packing to hold the pleats, but the process was so effective that surviving Delphos dresses in museums across the world remain as sharply creased as they ever were.

Clearly, several tenets of minimalism are inherent in Fortuny's Delphos dress. Its simple structure of flat shift with a bateau neckline and

Such neoclassical paintings as *Canaries* (1880s) by Albert Moore depicted fluid, free-flowing, draped clothing that promoted the comfort and ease of the wearer, inspiring Fortuny to create his Delphos dress.

it was very much a system of dressing with the piece at its heart, rather than a collection in any commercial sense.

In his blending of the Western neoclassical aesthetic with Eastern techniques, Fortuny was the first to practise the all-important cultural fusion that is at the heart of minimalist design. He drew from sources that would in turn be taken up in the 1970s and 1980s by Japanese designers Issey Miyake (whose own pleated pieces owe much to Fortuny's pioneering work) and Yohji Yamamoto.

Orientalism was at the heart of both Poiret's success and his failure. In 1905, while still an assistant at the House of Worth, he presented a new design known as the Confucius coat to a valued customer, the Russian Princess Bariatinsky:

Today it would seem banal but then nothing like it had been seen. It was a great square kimono in black cloth, bordered with black satin cut obliquely; the sleeves were wide right to the bottom and were finished with embroidered cuffs like those of Chinese mantles. 'Ah! What a horror,' she cried. 'With us, when there are low fellows who run after our sledges and annoy us, we have their heads cut off and we put them in sacks just like that.'[3]

While Poiret's Parisian designs successfully borrowed the Eastern simplicity of shape, and led to a more streamlined silhouette for womenswear, with fewer ruffles, flounces and trimmings, tastes had not yet evolved to accept the corresponding simplicity of aspect, and Poiret's orientalism took a direction of sumptuous brights, intricate beading and embroidery, and hyperbolic structural adornment.

Poiret's resurrection of Directoire style – a straighter, Empire-style line characterized by drapery and layering – was a triumph at least over the grip of the corset. Its original incarnation had been as a somewhat contrarian look adopted by a few influential belles between 1798 and 1805, before they abandoned it for a more gilded and ornamental style. But Poiret's Cairo tunic of

POIRET

1925: As the tunic – seen right in coat form – became popular, the waist became less of a focal point. Women were freed from their whalebone corsets, and a busy, urban existence became a real possibility.

1913: Poiret's designs for the theatre (far right) pioneered a freedom of movement that came from clothing less rigidly structured than usual; in his 'Zouave' dress, structure is created through draping and folding, by following the exigencies of the fabric.

POIRET

1919: The hobble skirt (right) was the first step in the evolution from full-length, floor-sweeping dresses, heralding a narrowing silhouette. Hobble skirts were often restrictively tight and not very practical, but they were simpler than what had come before.

Poiret's fondness for drama and luxurious embellishment (far right) means his designs are not inherently minimalist, but his simplification of the silhouette and separates of feminine dressing shows a certain purity of design.

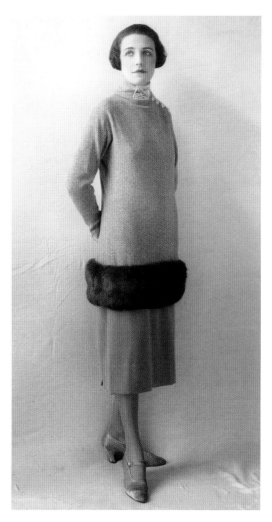

POIRET

1925: Separates became
de rigueur in womenswear,
as in menswear. Poiret's
favoured tunic shape
(right) was the catalyst
for a trend for layering
knits on shift dresses.

1927: Designers began
to feminize traditional
masculine pieces, such as
tailored suits and shirts,
creating collars and blouses
that looked softer than
their masculine equivalents
(right, bottom). Poiret's
swing coats became
cropped jackets, and his
hobble skirts chic sheaths.

1907, inspired by an ancient Athenian wedding dress, as well as his car coats, structural, cropped lampshade tunics and *jupes rattrapées* (hobble skirts), realigned notions of modern elegance practically overnight. The commercial potential was obvious, with a Worth dress selling for more than 5000 francs, and Poiret's less restrictive and more sober and versatile tunics priced at 700.

But the derided Confucius coat is a poignant synecdoche for Poiret's career: his design was an ingenious premise of what was to come, for which consumers were not ready. He concentrated meanwhile on expressing the spirit of his age in his theatrical and extravagant way, meaning that he became a catalyst for change rather than the arbiter of it. The exigencies of the First World War meant that the exotic and excessive look that he had so carefully constructed became irrelevant, and when he tried to revive it in peacetime, he too was placed in that category.

At the same time as Poiret was presenting his Cairo pieces, Gabrielle 'Coco' Chanel (1883–1971) was living with her patron, Étienne Balsan, reworking her plain-line outfits with masculine touches: a small bow tie here, a dartless, loose-fitting shirt there. Photographs from 1908 show her unencumbered alongside others in ungainly S-bend corsets and Henri II-style ruffs; under her ensemble, Chanel herself is wearing a simple 'modestie' slip, trimmed only with ribbon rather than with the requisite lace and pearls.

Living as Balsan's mistress and spending languid weekends in the country with the likes of music-hall actress Émilienne d'Alençon, Chanel rebelled against the stereotype of a 'kept woman', not wishing to seem the frilly, frothy flibbertigibbet, and paring her appearance down to the utmost basics. She dressed with a view to the day when a purism of appearance would prevail, an age when, to paraphrase her own words, women no longer functioned as an excuse for the use of ribbons, laces and embellishments.

Setting herself up as a milliner in 1910 on the rue Cambon in Paris, Chanel targeted excess from

POIRET

1925: By the 1920s womenswear had become less form-fitting and restrictive. Designers began to generate decoration from within the form of clothing, as in the case of these tiers (opposite), rather than from added extras.

CHANEL

1926: The designs of Coco Chanel rehabilitated black in the feminine wardrobe beyond mourning dress, with the popularization of the Little Black Dress (right) for day- and eveningwear.

the very top, as it were. Women's headgear had literally reached dizzying heights, with feathers, plumes and whole historic tableaux re-enacted on hats and bonnets. One reported piece of advice to fashionable women was not to waste overripe fruit or vegetables, but instead to arrange them artfully on the brim of a hat so as to make the most of them. 'It was grotesque', Chanel said. 'How could a brain function under all that?'[4] Hats 'were covered in foliage, flowers, fruits, feathers and ribbons,' noted Poiret, 'and excess in matters of fashion is a sign of the end'.[5]

Indeed, Chanel's view of contemporary womenswear in general was that it was as deliquescent as the fruit on everyone's hats. Her simple boaters and cloches were the first strike against extravagance, and when she opened her first boutique in Deauville in 1913, it stocked the clothes that she had been creating for herself for years. Suddenly everybody else wanted to wear them: the aristocrats who flocked to the coastal town during the war were looking for comfortable clothes in which they could promenade. A feeling of austerity, combined with a troubled economy and less formal attitudes, meant that her pieces – made in an entirely new style, inspired by masculine wardrobes and intended for living and moving in – were perfect. Until then, the etiquette had been to go to the beach in the same clothes that one would wear around the city; pictures of suited gentlemen and starched, laced ladies perched on the sand show quite clearly the death knells of a society founded on formality and aspiring to inactivity and impracticality.

Not, of course, that Chanel's range was at all bourgeois; it was still at the forefront of exclusive fashion, with dresses in her Biarritz couture house in 1916 retailing at 3000 francs each. Her fabrics, however, were a revelation to those who bought and wore them. Tricot – a material previously used only for underwear because it was thought to be too soft and of too poor a quality for tailoring – answered perfectly to the minimal treatment it received at the hands of

Chanel's seamstresses and the physically active lifestyle of the woman who put her name on its label. Chanel also introduced cotton jersey and flannel, more fabrics that would not have responded well to the flourishes and curlicues of Worth, Jeanne Paquin or Poiret, but the very durability and elasticity of which underscored the departure her clothes made from theirs.

A three-quarter-length coat made entirely from jersey was uncompromising in its lack of embellishment and its masculine severity, while 'vest-cut' jackets and dresses (that is, pieces that unbutton and open in the style of a man's jacket) and her obliteration of waistlines made Chanel's clothes ideal for the women liberated by the war, who went out alone in flat shoes and roamed the city in shorter skirts, in which they could

Less is ... New

1928: Princess Carla Boncampagni Ludovisi (below) in a sleeveless chiffon evening gown with a two-tiered skirt and draped fabric at the back. Chanel's glamour was significantly more subtle than the frou-frou of the 1910s.

1954: Inspired by the traditional masculine wardobe (below, right), Chanel subverted suiting and tailoring to create a more relaxed capsule of female garments.

actually walk a distance. After armistice and the reopening of channels of communication, women across the world were shocked by the presence of bare ankles in Paris; within a year, they were visible everywhere.

Chanel not only changed the landscape of fashion, but also to some extent redesigned that of the female body. Where clothing had previously emphasized bosom, waist and rump, hers did not cling at all, giving only a suggestion of the body that lay beneath, while letting that body work as fully as it was naturally intended to, unconstrained by hoops, petticoats and lacing. The feminine paradigm shifted from the shorter, more curvaceous French archetype to a slimmer and taller, more athletic shape. 'Formerly women were architectural,' complained Poiret in 1927, 'like the prows of ships, and very beautiful. Now they resemble little undernourished telegraph clerks ... What has Chanel invented? Poverty de luxe.'[6]

Chanel's decision to work mainly in monochrome gave women a seriousness they had never had, one that they had not recognized was possible when Princess Bariatinsky rejected the Confucius coat, but one that Chanel deemed strictly necessary. Even by the time such designers as Elsa Schiaparelli were working, during the

1930s, with fuchsia and organdie and trousers cropped at the calf, Chanel obstinately refused to create anything that was not cut along the masculine line, tailored sharply (but not rigidly) and sombre in tone.

The American Look

France – and Europe – had indeed been through sobering times, but they retained after the First World War a broader sense of social structure and cultural elitism; the United States, on the other hand, had nothing resembling that existing hierarchy, priding itself on the tangibility of the American Dream and the potential for Everyman to rise as high as he wished. Bound up in this was the need to expand the consumer market through appeals to utilitarianism and egalitarianism, which gained momentum only during the Depression of the 1930s, when the fledgling American fashion industry found itself working to a pared-down, workwear-inspired aesthetic. Where the minimalist approaches and revolutions in style made by Fortuny, Poiret and Chanel had been done with a righteous cultural integrity, they had also come from an artistic – and therefore intellectual – standpoint. America's early versions of minimalism had a broader focus.

Minimalism in the United States was almost the complete antithesis, in fact, of the simplification of dress that had happened in Europe, where a version of sportswear had been created for the leisured classes; such American designers as Claire McCardell (1905–1958), Vera Maxwell (1901–1995) and Clare Potter (1903–1999), under the auspices of such larger distributing brands as Townley, Norell and Hattie Carnegie, created a kind of leisurewear for the working class – or at least for the broader middle classes. ('Sportswear' in this context refers not to clothes specifically designed for exercise – although they could often be worn for that – but to casualwear and untailored pieces.) The key

1952: McCardell borrowed
from the masculine wardrobe
the notion of workable and
interchangeable separates
(left). She created a
functional range of essential,
basic pieces all designed to
be mixed and matched – the
first capsule wardrobe.

1949: Mrs R. Fulton Cutting II
(left, bottom) in a simple
wool shirt dress with a plain
circle skirt; oversized breast
pockets and cuffs are the
only embellishment.

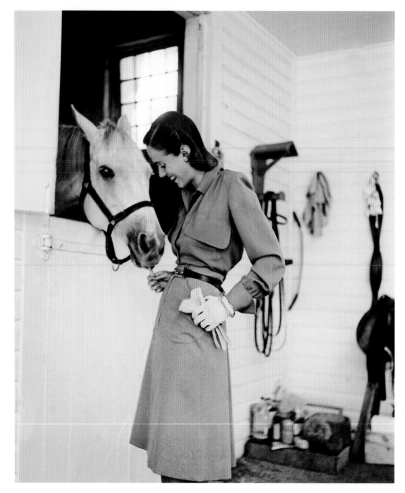

targets were white, middle-class college girls,
housewives and working women – essentially,
almost all walks of feminine life.

Technological advances in mass production
meant that the manufacture of cheap garments
had become easier, as long as the pieces were
simple enough to reproduce on a large scale and
did not require too many panels to be cut out.
McCardell and Potter saw that as a challenge,
using their ingenuity to integrate stylish design
with functional simplicity, of the kind sought by
the wearer in an everyday garment, as well as
that needed by manufacturers to keep costs to
a minimum. It was the first acknowledgement of
the correlation between sartorial and commercial
pragmatism, factors that would become very
important in the growth and popularity of
minimalist design.

American fashion – then, as now, based on
Seventh Avenue in New York – took the line that
clothes-buying was as patriotic an act as any
other, and so fashion became imbued with
a righteous fervour of the type seen in Nazi-
occupied Paris during the Second World War, at
the German proposal that all couture workshops
should be moved to Vienna. After the toll taken on
the American Dream by the Depression and the
war, Seventh Avenue-made clothes became a
means of expressing not only national identity but
also national spirit, an indefatigable American
optimism regardless of adversity. Simple lines and
functional, durable fabrics became emblematic
of a national willingness to endure and overcome
hardship; a practical reliance on 'classic'
garments was sold to consumers as a stolid,
American virtue of not being swayed by the
superficial or superfluous.

Buoying the reputation of simplicity in dress
and the enduring practicality of minimalist
pieces was key in so large a market as the United
States, where spontaneous, flimsy trends would
not sell in large enough numbers to make them
a viable commercial prospect. Again, we see the
reliance on basics, essentials and a fundamental

CLAIRE MCCARDELL

1946: The rise of American
sportswear was inextricably
linked to the broadening
of women's existence: they
needed simple, elegant
clothing appropriate to their
new-found level of activity,
whether for work or leisure.
McCardell's shantung
dresses (seen on the model
in the foreground) were
ideal for either.

Less is ... New

TINA LESER

1945: A smocked coat in
the monastic style (below,
foreground). The model in
the background wears a
similarly austere suit-shaped
coat by Monte-Sano.

CLAIRE MCCARDELL

1946: McCardell designed
with mass production in
mind, creating dresses from
as few panels of material as
possible (opposite); often her
clothes were dartless and
seamless, their shape and
structure created instead by
the natural fall of the fabric.

system of dressing, an approach similar to that
of Fortuny and reworked by Calvin Klein and
Donna Karan, whose American national identity
is intrinsic to their brand identity. If an item sold
well, it would be retained for countless seasons
and brought out in various colours with minor
adaptations; these themes originated with Mildred
Orrick (1906–1994) and Vera Maxwell in the
1930s. During the same decade, Claire McCardell
produced a collection of six interchangeable
garments, intended to be purchased together to
give the modern woman a coordinated wardrobe
of a few separates that could be worn in several
combinations to produce various outfits. Where
Chanel and Fortuny sought to change and
simplify the overall look of the twentieth-century
woman, American sportswear designers aimed
to change and simplify her life, from her shopping
habits to the very way she got dressed.

Of course, these practical changes were
informed by larger political ones: the limitations
imposed by the technology of production, as
discussed, for one, but also the effect of rationing
during the Second World War, and the changes in
lifestyle imposed by the conflict. Whereas during
the First World War the women of Paris had
needed garb that readied them for the reality of
walking in the streets, American women in the
1930s needed clothes that could cover every
eventuality, from childcare to office work to
leisure time. New York sportswear designers
followed principles of anonymity and ambiguity
in their pieces, that their clothes might work in
any of these scenarios. The shirtwaister dress
by Tina Leser (1910–1986), for example – the
next incarnation of Poiret's tunics – was a longer-
length shirt, cut to emphasize the shape of the
body and belted at the waist to create a smart,
multi-purpose piece that both wives and workers
could appropriate for their own uses.

Likewise, Vera Maxwell's skirt suit of 1937
was a masterpiece in the elimination of all
details extra to its needs: the collarless neckline
was decorated only by a row of triple-stitching;

Less is ... New

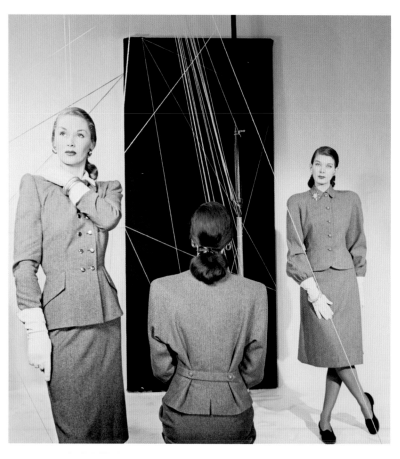

VERA MAXWELL

1946: Wartime rationing rendered suiting austere, but designers adapted their style to such severities. Maxwell's tailoring (on the left and right) is cut on the bias so that shape comes from the fabric itself, and sleeves, collars and cuffs are integral to the cut, rather than extras. The centre suit is by Capri.

embellishment came in the form of a contrast between the diagonal weave of the bias-cut fabric and the rib of the hem. Such plain pieces may have played to a national sense of moral abstemiousness, but they also gave women a more serious image, for the same reason that Chanel remained in thrall to monochrome for so long. Between 1930 and 1940, the number of women in the American workforce rose by more than 25 per cent;[7] dealing with a feminine presence in the workplace was a challenge for men and women alike, but restrained clothing was seen to be one method of handling each gender's perceived discomfort.

This restraint led to a vogue for austere clothing. Although fashion and film rarely collided at this point, there was a trend for elegantly stark medievalism in Hollywood during the late 1930s and early 1940s, and that coincided with the launch of Claire McCardell's Monastic dress, an over-the-head woollen number free from any external embellishments, but constructed in a way belied by its external simplicity. Rather than using understructures or padding, McCardell shaped the dress from its cut alone: sleeve shape emphasized the shoulders, while a bias-cut bodice gave contouring, and a full-circle skirt allowed for volume and a whittled waist with none of the usual corsetry or underskirts. McCardell's next success was for Townley in 1938: the Nada dress, meaning – quite intentionally – 'nothing'. The advertisement boasted of its simple complexities: 'An entirely new silhouette ... An ageless, dateless silhouette, simple as a monk's cassock, regal as a king's robe! ... a design that might have come from the master hand of a Vionnet. Flaring straight from the shoulders in soft folds gathered in a wide belt to make your waist look tiny ... It fits everyone ... it's comfortable, it's versatile – appropriate for business or tea!'[8] While simplicity in French couture was considered a virtue of the wearer's deep-seated ability to appreciate design, the American approach emphasized its respectability and intrinsic moral qualities.

1948: A model in a typical
shirt dress. Buttons and
waist-height pleating
are functional and
structural, as well as
moderately decorative.

Less is ... New

1949: The ultimately practical persona of American sportswear (right) derived from a sense of 'making do' during and after the war; its designers were inspired by the work women did during the war, and many pieces had a military or uniform aesthetic.

CLAIRE MCCARDELL

1942: The cotton 'popover' dress (far right; The Metropolitan Museum of Art, New York) was a wraparound style, cut in two pieces and fastened with buttons – decorative in themselves – along the side of the body; there is a quilted patch pocket on one side of the skirt and a matching oven mitt, which attaches to the waistband by a tape.

CLAIRE MCCARDELL

1946: Made from such light, durable fabrics as cotton and jersey, McCardell's dresses were everyday basics for most women (opposite, bottom left). Her few nods to decoration came from functional extras, such as the thick straps and small, frilled peplum of this sundress.

1946: The rise of the one-piece bodysuit and bathing suit (opposite, bottom right) was seen as the ultimate fusion of fashion and function: a wardrobe solution with something futuristic about its great practicality.

When the Second World War began, of course, there was rationing to consider, and the L-85 regulations introduced by the War Production Board in 1942 attempted to restrict yardage in the clothing industry by introducing what was known as 'the silhouette': a simplicity of design and detailed breakdowns of cloth allowance according to size. 'Clothes must be simple,' announced US *Vogue* in September 1942, 'that's the government rule – but hasn't it always been your personal Golden Rule?'[9] Rationing restrictions meant further limitations for such designers as McCardell and Potter, but it was yet another challenge to which they rose ably. 'Most of my ideas come from trying to solve my own problems', said McCardell in an interview, referencing her own womanhood much as Chanel had done when defending her design strategy.[10]

Indeed, the American sportswear designers were crucial when it came to the war effort, with Muriel King (1900–1977) creating a range of aircraft workers' uniforms in 1943 and Hattie Carnegie (1889–1956) producing military nursing uniforms. Their unique talents for combining a utilitarian aesthetic with the practicalities of production were valuable assets in these straitened times. McCardell's denim 'popover' dress of 1942 was the ultimate synthesis of form and fashion from the era: a simply cut dress designed for women who had lost their home help to the war effort, it comprised a bodice cut in two pieces, crossing each other diagonally to create a wrapover effect and fastening with McCardell's signature white buttons. These buttons provided what appeared to be decoration but were intrinsic to the dress's construction, and, in what was perhaps the ultimate fusion of form, function and femininity, the dress came with a detachable oven glove.

But while such examples prove the extent to which wartime fashions were anchored to concurrent notions of womanly deportment, the overall changes in feminine apparel during the period were undeniable. By 1943, famed editor

Diana Vreeland was championing Mildred Orrick's prototype leotard in *Harper's Bazaar*; such a garment, with so unerring a focus on versatility and freedom of movement, would have been unthinkable even twenty years previously.

Notes
1 Quoted by Yvonne Deslandres in *Poiret: Paul Poiret, 1879–1944*, London (Thames & Hudson) 1987, p. 149.
2 Paul Poiret, *My First Fifty Years*, London (Gollancz) 1931, p. 72.
3 *Ibid.*, pp. 65–66.
4 Quoted in Edmonde Charles-Roux, *Chanel and Her World*, London (n.p.) 1981, p. 96.
5 Poiret, *My First Fifty Years*, pp. 288–89.
6 Quoted in Charles-Roux, *Chanel and Her World*, p. 96.
7 Sharon Hartman Strom, *Beyond the Typewriter*, Urbana and Chicago (University of Illinois Press) 1992, p. 370.
8 Best & Co. advertisement, cited by Rebecca Arnold in *The American Look*, London (I.B. Tauris) 2009, p. 126.
9 'Autumn Openings', *Vogue* (US), 1 September 1942, p. 43.
10 Quoted in *Contemporary Fashion*, ed. Taryn Benbow-Pfalzgraf, Detroit (St James Press) 2002, p. 461.

Less is ... Couture

A New Minimalist Elegance, 1945–57

CHRISTIAN DIOR

1949: Dior's hyper-feminine clothes were striking in their architecture, maximal in their effect but minimal in their aesthetic. Femininity did not necessarily mean a return to frou-frou.

The developments in womenswear before the Second World War highlight the dichotomy in the advance of minimalist design: on the one hand, the intellectual use of simplicity in fashion, and on the other, its necessity in practical terms. No one could say that Chanel's garments were not practical, of course, but they arose from a considered and somewhat cerebral take on dress, and did not – at first – make much impact on the working woman. Clothes made by the likes of Vera Maxwell and Claire McCardell, however, were born of necessity, fulfilling the needs of buyer and manufacturer alike. Although the impetus for each was different, the new direction was at least the product of a general sense that, as Paul Poiret put so well, 'excess in matters of fashion is a sign of the end'.[1]

But with the end of the war, in America at least, there was no immediate backtracking to the use of more fabric, more embellishment, more of everything. Rationing was, after all, still in place. At a luncheon held by the Fashion Group (a not-for-profit organization set up in 1930 to tackle problems within the industry) in 1943, Jessica Daves, the editor of US Vogue, gave a slideshow, describing not only the virtues of American sportswear but also, perhaps, the best way to market it to buyers. 'A narrow silhouette with nearly-normal shoulders; arm-sized sleeves, or none; and almost knee-length skirts', she said. 'It would be a mistake to call this new look of clothes "simplicity". It is really a triumph of premeditated elimination.'[2] It was the first instance in which the sportswear aesthetic had been credited as a design movement in itself rather than simply a commercial industry that answered the practical needs of the market.

Vogue, and Seventh Avenue more widely, began to imbue the American Look, as it became known, with a righteous quality of denial. The pared-down aesthetic became morally commendable, with Vogue's issue of January 1945 urging readers to 'unclutter' their lives: 'The difference between clutter and unclutter is the difference between

order and disorder. Unclutter is not merely emptiness; it is arrangement ... It means, in the best sense, the achievement of simplicity out of complexity.'[3] This is perhaps one of the first invocations of minimalism as a spiritual comfort; its use as a means of controlling at least one aspect of lifestyle and its potential for stoic denial would become central to its popularity (or indeed its unpopularity), but Vogue's post-war standpoint once again brings attention to the practicalities of the look and its development in harmony with this specific zeitgeist.

Minimalism was also presented as a forward-looking movement. Without yet having accrued some of the science-fiction elements that have become inherent in modern minimalism, it was nonetheless allied with the march of progress. Mildred Orrick's leotard was compared to a costume from the Flash Gordon comic strip when it launched, and many of McCardell's designs were deemed rather avant-garde for contemporary audiences. A Vogue photoshoot positions one of her pieces within a starkly Modernist Robsjohn-Gibbings interior, while advertisements of the era from such companies as Norell and Townley position models not on the streets of the city, but cut-out and floating in a liminal white space to accentuate notions of timelessness. The tone of these adverts was still gung-ho, still avowedly optimistic about the idealism and normality of simplicity and functionalism.

It seems almost unfathomable, then, after such a scaling-back of resources and taste, that in February 1947 Christian Dior (1905–1957) would show Parisian audiences a circle-cut skirt almost 20 metres (66 ft) in circumference. The arrival of the 'New Look' was startling, both to ladies of fashion, retailers and the press, who had seen nothing like it for a long time, and to the public, who deemed it obscene, given that rationing was still nominally in place. Despite the praise heaped on sportswear designers for their ingenuity, Dior's first collection was hailed as

Less is ... Couture

CLAIRE MCCARDELL

1957: American sportswear became imbued with an optimism and enthusiasm for simplicity and paring back (right), and was presented as a contrast to the elaborate and luxurious wares coming from the Paris couture houses.

After the war, sportswear was heralded as a design movement in itself (right, bottom), rather than a commercial directive that had answered the practical needs of the market during the difficult war years.

1929: Actor Helen Lyons (right) in an asymmetrical coat by Vionnet. The designer's signature bias cut gave clothes her trademark drape and a fluidity of expression that precluded the need for further embellishment.

1931: Many of Vionnet's pieces, such as this black cape (right, bottom), were cut from a single piece of fabric, minimally treated at the hands of the designer in order to realize the potential of the material.

an end to the ugliness of wartime clothing and a much-needed divergence from the perceived pre-war direction of haute couture.

Inter-war Developments: Vionnet and Balenciaga

In the designs of Poiret and Chanel, couture had engaged with the onset of Modernism with simpler lines and by introducing and developing a more minimal type of elegance; whether fashion would have taken that direction had the two wars not occurred is naturally impossible to say, but the work of Madeleine Vionnet (1876–1975) and Cristóbal Balenciaga (1895–1972), as well as many elements present in that definitive Dior collection, suggest that minimalism in fashion was undeniably integral to the industry's progression both pre- and post-war.

Vionnet's work in the 1920s and 1930s can be aligned with that of Chanel, although the two women disliked each other and were keen to distance themselves and their creations. They share, however, a similar intent of naturalism and restraint in dress: Chanel took a sports-based approach to elegance, hand-picking elements of the masculine wardrobe, while Vionnet owed more to the classical lines explored by Fortuny and the Aesthetic movement, and the importance of clothing as filled by the body in all its kinetic potential.

By draping fabric on the bias – that is, with the weft and weave running diagonally rather than vertically and horizontally – Vionnet was able to create and manipulate a certain amount of elasticity and 'give' in the materials with which she worked. It ensured a more fluid and flattering look to the piece, which would hang in natural folds rather than appearing flatter, as did clothes not made on the bias. This cut was fundamental to her design aesthetic and to her deliberately pared-down look, providing as it did fullness, shape and weight while obviating the need for

any embellishment. Bias-cut pieces use up to double the amount of cloth of non-bias garments, so Vionnet's minimalist approach was far from thrifty or egalitarian, but her eminently – and quietly – luxurious pieces gave new credence in the movement to upmarket buyers looking for the very best but not necessarily the very brash.

Vionnet was a dedicated modernizer of fashion, working first of all in miniature and experimenting with fit and drape on dolls rather than life-sized mannequins. This allowed her to develop her methods of working around the body rather than viewing it from head to toe, working in three dimensions rather than a flat, linear progression.

This should be recognized as an important facet of minimalism: not only the consideration of the body and its ability to move within clothes (which can be viewed more largely as functionalism), but also the technique of working in the round, another link to Japanese technique and tradition.

While Japanese clothing, stereotypically and traditionally, is based on flat-cut patterns and simple panelled pieces that lack the volume and fullness of, say, a more typically Western circle skirt or nineteenth-century bodice, it is generally considered and conceived in lifelike dimensions. A value for volume and asymmetry, for example, appears more regularly in the history of kimono

1931: This stylized portrait (opposite) of a model in Vionnet's signature crêpe pyjamas recalls the classical essence of her designs and the similarities between her aesthetic and that of Fortuny and the revivalists.

1937: Working foremost with the exigencies of the fabric and the body of the wearer in mind, Vionnet's pared-down pieces – such as this lambskin-lined collarless coat (right) – were fluid and flawless.

design than in the annals of Western dress. The Japanese have a heritage of working around the body, rather than sketching first the front and then the back of a dress, an approach that often places artistry before technical appreciation, motion or progression. When one is working to the body's code rather than to that of the beholder, pieces take on a sort of autonomy that can be linked to a minimalist aesthetic, because the basic needs of the wearer are laid bare. McCardell's pieces created with a view to ease of manufacturing exemplify this, made as they are from panels that interlock to form the whole piece, rather than producing a whole look born of disparate elements.

It was, however, the lack of panelling or planes in a Vionnet dress that gave it an absolutist aspect, a continuity around the body without complication or interruption. 'A Vionnet looks like nothing in the hand', wrote Bruce Chatwin more than thirty years after the designer retired. 'It contains no artificial stiffening and flops limply on the hanger.'[4] While her creations were conspicuous by their lack of adornment and, apparently, of substance, they were also revolutionary in their simplicity, and scandalous at times because they came with no linings or understructures, and were often sheer on the wearer's body.

In fact, where Chanel had subverted the uniform of men for her work, Vionnet transposed the vocabulary of lingerie on to hers, avoiding intrusion into her chosen fabrics, wrapping, draping and hanging without darts or shaping wherever possible, and creating structure from the manipulation of fabric. Her pieces were bought and studied assiduously by McCardell and other sportswear designers, who attempted to translate them for mass consumption, and whose incorporation of stitching, seamwork, drawstrings and other structurally crucial elements as decoration can also be traced to the earlier work of Vionnet.

Structurally, Vionnet's pieces owe much to the chitons that inspired Mariano Fortuny, and their sculptural nature takes us back also to the statue from which the idea for the Delphos dress came. But Fortuny's work, revolutionary as it was, created an overall sense of minimalism and the sculptural, while on closer inspection his dresses could be seen to be the work of a conceptual working artist rather than that of a skilled couturier. His pattern-cutting skills were not on a par with those of Vionnet, who is often cited as the greatest cutter in the history of dress; given that her chosen medium was not in tailoring, this is a plaudit indeed, as her cuts provided a shell for the body, rather than sartorial armour for it. It is this sense of the complexities of simplicity, as discussed by *Vogue*'s Jessica Daves in 1943 (see p. 35), that makes Vionnet so crucial to minimalism in fashion: her 'premeditated elimination' of all extraneous elements and strict focus on construction.

The fact that she worked primarily – although not relentlessly – in black lends Vionnet's work

Less is ... Couture

1955: Balenciaga's clothes were plain but sculptural, with any adornment taking on a near-architectural quality, as in this cape with a ruffled yoke (right).

1946: Balenciaga's signature blacks and form-skirting silhouette (right, bottom) became synonymous with Parisian style in the 1940s.

1951: Three models in Balenciaga dresses inspired by the artist Henri de Toulouse-Lautrec (opposite); the sculptural qualities of the gowns and their silhouettes are shown to best advantage through Balenciaga's stark juxtaposition of black and vivid colour.

further relevance to minimalism. It was not unfamiliar territory, of course, considering Chanel's contemporaneous and almost exclusive use of the shade, but the rival designer was working mainly in tailoring and masculine-inspired womenswear, and Vionnet's pieces were far more traditionally feminine in style. Given the reputation of couture as a modernizing force at that time, consumers were no longer afraid of wearing black, and reactions similar to that of Princess Bariatinsky to Poiret's coat (see p. 19) were rare after 1920.

Such was the integration of black into fashionable society – and it was formerly worn only by the bereaved and the poor – that by 1937, when Cristóbal Balenciaga opened his couture house in Paris, the shade was considered quite the mark of chic. Balenciaga's use of black is often attributed to his Spanish heritage and Catholic upbringing; in fact, his work displays aspects of the monastic and medieval throughout, and black is merely one manifestation of his brand of sumptuous minimalism. 'This is the black of Spain,' said an article in *Harper's Bazaar* in 1938, 'so deep in tone that all other blacks seem grey beside it.'[5]

While much of Balenciaga's work may be eye-catching and flamboyant in style, it is also characterized by an austerity and restraint that informs the overall aesthetic. As the designer explained to a young Hubert de Givenchy, in the days when they worked together, context is all: 'There are different kinds of ruffles', he said. 'Some ruffles must be very, very elegant and light you know. You must make it become an intelligent ruffle.'[6] The notion of ruffles should be anathema to any designer working in a minimalist vein, but Balenciaga's restrained use of extras is the first example of a developed sort of minimalism, one that is coherent enough in its vision to incorporate and benefit from additions and decorative leitmotifs. The exaggerated yokes on coats, the ruched gathering on tube skirts and melon sleeves, the flared cuffs of fitted jackets: each is in harmony with the piece on which it appears,

Less is ... Couture

BALENCIAGA

1938: Balenciaga mixed body-consciousness with volume (top left) to create shapes that would preoccupy many later minimalists.

1954: This trapeze-line tweed coat (top right) is devoid of embellishment except for the functional – and barely visible – pockets on the sleeves.

1950: Balenciaga's famous 'melon sleeves' (bottom left) were created by ruching and folding wool velour, and came to symbolize his hyperbolic structural style.

1953: Balenciaga became preoccupied by the search for the perfect sleeve (bottom right). Here, a pair of knotted white-satin cuffs, worn with a Hattie Carnegie dress, shows his striving to create structure and form by working with nothing but the cloth itself.

in single block colours on such sturdy fabrics as faille and gazar, an expensive silk produced exclusively for the house.

While Balenciaga might not be singularly categorized as a minimalist designer – consider his later lace pieces, his appliqué flowers, the warning he was given for overly adorned hats during wartime rationing – he is certainly a designer motivated by minimalism. One of the signature shapes with which he worked from the beginning of his career to the end (and which, in fact, signalled the end of his career rather emphatically through its adoption by younger designers as a minidress) was the T-shaped tunic, whether in dress form or as a top. As in the case of Poiret and the American Look, the tunic could be multifariously adapted and was a cornerstone for designers concerned with creating simplified and unpretentious clothing because of the adaptations of silhouette it so readily facilitated. Balenciaga showed retooled tunics in 1956, and in following years reworked the shape to create his infamous 'sacque' dresses, architectural and voluminous pieces designed to skim the form of the body and free it for movement, while maintaining that elegance of silhouette for which couturiers of the era are known.

Balenciaga introduced a new architecture to clothes, creating shape, volume and structure that had not been seen since the days of the bustle and hooped skirt. But he created his structures, just as Vionnet did, by working with the vagaries of his materials, rather than adding anything to them. 'Balenciaga was a revelation to me,' Givenchy said, 'because he never chose the facile solution. In one of his ensembles with just a single seam in the middle of the back, the line was so pure, so clear, that it conveyed simplicity in its very perfection. When one realized that everything stemmed from the line of the body, that the fabrics themselves were vibrantly alive, simplicity became a form of great art.'[7] One such manifestation of Balenciaga's drive for harmony and perfection is his lifelong preoccupation with

the cut of sleeves. When commentators saw his collection for Spring/Summer 1939, they marvelled at sleeves that were cut into the square yoke of a coat, one half forming the front and the other the back, with all the flat-cut simplicity of a kimono.

Balenciaga's innate elegance took inspiration from Eastern dress and construction, with his single-seam tailored pieces that were structured only by a carefully placed series of darts and tucks, and supplemented it with his own inherited sense of Spanish drama for dresses that billowed with air as the wearer moved, so that their true silhouette was revealed only by the body in motion. Neutral, earthy tones recalled Moorish Spain, while the more monastic of his designs were influenced by the religious paintings of such artists as Goya and Zurbarán; his floor-sweeping capes and yoked coats and dresses summon perfectly a sense of both the arcane and the modern, a balance that minimalist fashion often struggles to maintain. Vionnet's pieces, as we have seen, can be closely allied to the medium of sculpture, to the neoclassical folds of a chiton rendered in marble or granite, but Balenciaga was the first designer to create truly architectural clothes on a Modernist, if not quite Brutalist, wavelength.

Balenciaga's was a stark aesthetic, wilfully using minimalism to create a sense of hermetic closeness and exclusivity in a brand anonymity that reflected his own precious privacy and need to de-personalize his work. Working with the sculptor Janine Janette to create pieces for the window displays at his boutique on the avenue George V in Paris, Balenciaga was the first designer to attempt the creation of a determinedly minimalist brand; the stark windows and austere shops were supposed to reference the pared-down, 'thoughtful' clothing that was on sale there, once again giving the minimalist aesthetic a purifying or improving angle.

This inherent austerity can come across to many pundits as a self-righteous sort of droopiness at best, or intellectual snobbery

Less is ... Couture

at worst. But some of the most glamorous women of the 1950s wore Balenciaga's gowns to grand events, and his designs were considered to be among the finest occasionwear ever created, in terms both of skill and of their eminent ability to be photogenic.

However, after the Second World War there was undeniably a sense that fashion had been righteously impoverished for too long. It was this sentiment that lay behind Dior's iconic collection of 1947, the one that – according to legend – had women fighting in the streets. It is not unusual or impossible to predict that, after a period of hardship, those better placed to enjoy luxury once more seek it in conspicuous fashion. It had happened, as we have seen, during the First World War in Deauville, as the aristocracy flocked to buy Chanel's rather more exclusive version of practical clothing. But, given the rather sober and utilitarian aspect both wars had conferred on womenswear, in this instance those who could afford to be different wanted to be visibly, even recklessly, so.

The New Look

Dior overhauled the feminine silhouette, showing long, full skirts with long-line jackets cinched in over wasp waists. Erasing the hard work involved in eliminating the corset, the Parisian designer instigated once more complicated understructures of padding, boning and lacing. Eyewitnesses from that first show remember women in the audience wrapping themselves more tightly in their boxy jackets and tugging down the short hems of their war-issue skirts. Dior had sidestepped the natural evolution of a trend and brought in something completely unexpected. That is not out of step with the given qualities of minimalist work (be it art, architecture, interior design or clothing), one of which is to be visually arresting, displaying a tangible difference from other objects. What Dior gave Paris was certainly minimal in some ways, although it aimed for maximum effect.

The collection did not represent entirely a regression to the fussiness of the belle époque; after all, that instantly recognizable suit with its full black circle skirt and white jacket has none of the trimmings previously associated with women's daywear, nor is it essentially restrictive. Its luxury comes from the no-holds-barred approach to fabric yardage, its newness from the ultra-, if not hyper-, feminine silhouette.

This is yet another point at which to reaffirm Dior's place within a minimalist scheme of fashion during the twentieth century. His lines are as sculptural or as architectural as those of Vionnet or Balenciaga, similarly taking the female body as his directive. But Dior's interpretation of womenswear is just that: his. 'La robe doit suivre le corps de la femme, ce n'est pas la femme qui doit suivre la robe', said Balenciaga.[8] 'When a woman smiles, her dress should smile with her', said Vionnet.[9] 'Women, with their sure instinct, realized that my intention was to make them not just more beautiful but also happier', said Dior.[10] The first two designers preached the value of naturalism, the third anything but; femininity had gone to seed during the war, he argued, and artifice – in its artistic sense, rather than making a case for vanity – should not be dismissed out of hand.

Within the realm of minimalism there is, of course, no dictate that an object ought to be natural or as close as possible to its natural state. Consider the somewhat tortuous buildings by such architects as Le Corbusier and Frank Lloyd Wright (the latter's Guggenheim Museum in New York, for example). These buildings are pared-down and simple in structure but complex in construction. Balenciaga himself was not averse to padding the hips of a cocktail gown in order to create a certain silhouette; Dior took the procedure a little further and created some of the first non-natural minimalist clothing.

But how far from natural can Dior's clothes be, when they are hyperbolic representations of the female form? Those delicate waists, straight backs and undulating hips are exaggerated versions of

Less is ... Couture

CHRISTIAN DIOR

1947: Dior's New Look (right) ushered in a new rigidity of form and a hyper-feminine silhouette that had languished on the periphery since the advent of classical naturalism and sportswear.

1952: The New Look combined the drapery and elegance of Vionnet's clothes with the more modern, structured qualities of Balenciaga's (right, bottom).

1950: Once more, simple construction belies a complex appearance (opposite). Leaves of pleated white silk are layered to create a millefeuille dress bound with a yellow sash, an ultimately minimalist but hyper-feminine look.

what they cover. The impetus for minimalism in fashion had so far been the liberation of women from their clothes, and this had come – quite naturally – in the form of raiding the masculine wardrobe for inspiration, in the case of Chanel; creating pieces with a form dictated by the very person who wore it, in the case of Vionnet; using the bare minimum in terms of cloth and cut, as in the case of American sportswear; and loosening the received silhouette, as Balenciaga did. There simply had not been an instance of minimalism that had made full use of the natural curvilinear shapes of women. Dior's clothes had none of the extremism of the nineteenth century, but they had all of its nostalgia.

Arguments against too much femininity in minimalist clothing, therefore, owe something to the idea that the feminine form is in some way 'excessive'. The minimalist designer's mandate is not to create a yashmak or abaya; it is to generate a mode of simplicity within a recognizable realm of extant clothing, a mode conspicuous by being in some way 'less'. What Dior did was build on a by now well-established tradition of 'premeditated elimination', presenting it with a historicism that referred to and built on both starting point and progression. Consumers were ready to forget angles and geometry, the concrete and cubism that seemed so redolent of the totalitarian machines against which they had fought for survival, and they basked in the softness and romanticism, the distant familiarity, of Dior's New Look.

With both Dior and Balenciaga working in this mode, minimalism became less of an acquired taste, as it became obvious that real austerity was out, and sumptuous, luxurious simplicity was the order of the day. Elegance owed everything to taste and quality, meaning that even daywear and ready-to-wear pieces were informed by the aesthetic. In the United Kingdom, skirt suits by Hardy Amies (1909–2003) looked to the 1920s, with slightly dropped waists, straight jackets and long-line bodices; Edward Molyneux (1891–1974), too, was known for his natural restraint. In the

MOLYNEUX

1936: Edward Molyneux's signature tailoring was pared back and austere-looking, but with a certain feeling of luxury, born of sumptuous materials and bias cuts – as with this swing coat (right).

CHRISTIAN DIOR

1954: The introduction
of new silhouettes every
season meant that Dior's
vision of womenswear was
constantly evolving (right). In
this 'string bean' silhouette
a hobble skirt is offset by
drapery and swagging at
the hip to create structure.

1951: Stiffer fabrics, such
as the taffeta of this dinner
ensemble (below), allowed
Dior to create new silhouettes
without most of the restrictive
underpinnings of early
twentieth-century fashions.

March 1950 issue of British *Vogue*, a pale-grey
flannel swing-coat is pictured, with the caption:
'These clothes are good-mannered; they seldom
trumpet their qualities; but they are clothes that
elegant women everywhere love to possess.'[11]

Such qualities were of the utmost importance
when elegance was the desired expression of the
day, but with the 1960s came new notions of self-
expression, of what was elegant and what was
downright tired. Balenciaga's favoured tunic
shapes made a reappearance on all sides, with
Dior developing the 'H-line' shift of the mid-
1950s and the designer himself reworking it for
1957, to create the tobacco-brown wool tunic
worn provocatively short by a model on the cover
of *L'Officiel*. Against a stark, clean background,
she looked every bit the woman of the future: the
tunic, the simplistic garment of re-invention, had
become the minidress. And there were several
pattern-cutters ready to experiment with it: one,
Pierre Cardin, who had worked for Dior and was
about to launch his own line; another, working
under Balenciaga, named André Courrèges; and a
third, Dior's right-hand man, Yves Saint Laurent.

Notes
 1 Paul Poiret, *My First Fifty Years*, London (Gollancz) 1931,
   pp. 288–89.
 2 Quoted in 'Lauds Fashions of Today', *New York Times*,
   20 November 1943, p. 10.
 3 'Unclutter', *Vogue* (US), 1 January 1945, p. 86.
 4 Bruce Chatwin, 'Surviving in Style', *Sunday Times
   Magazine*, 4 March 1973.
 5 Cited in Marie-Andrée Jouve, *Balenciaga*, London (Thames
   & Hudson) 1989, p. 34.
 6 Quoted in Myra Walker, *Balenciaga and His Legacy*,
   New Haven, Conn. (Yale University Press) 2006, p. 4.
 7 Quoted in *ibid*., p. 133.
 8 'The dress should follow the woman's body, the woman
   shouldn't have to follow the dress'. Quoted in *ibid*., p. 4;
   present author's translation.
 9 Quoted in *Contemporary Fashion*, ed. Taryn Benbow-
   Pfalzgraf, Detroit (St James Press) 2002, p. 702.
10 Quoted in Marie-France Pochna, *Dior*, London (Thames
   & Hudson) 1996, p. 4.
11 'The London Way', *Vogue* (UK), March 1950, p. 77.

Less is ... Modern

A Pared-Down Idiom for the Space Age, 1957–76

PIERRE CARDIN

1969: Cardin's collections were characterized by a functional asceticism; his clothes were notable in the 1960s for having no frills or frou-frou embellishment.

By January 1962, *Vogue* was ringing the changes and celebrating the newly simplified direction that fashion was taking: 'What's been coming for a long time has now arrived: the Thirties look, comprising all the sterling shapes of shifty, flirty skirts, semi-fitted coats, long, lean torsos ... Now's the time to sell your mink for an acre of pale grey flannel.'[1]

There was a sense that fashion's evolution was long overdue: the hierarchical system of couturiers and customers was beginning to seem outmoded as the pressures of the oncoming Youthquake began to make themselves known. There was a great need – and desire – among the young for something new, thrilling and different, something that was not part of the hegemony to which their parents belonged, something that existed only for them. It seems quite appropriate, then, that out of the *ancien régime* came the new blood: Pierre Cardin, André Courrèges and Yves Saint Laurent, each at one time apprenticed to some of the greatest established names in the industry, but no longer content to work under somebody else's aegis.

Cardin (born 1922) had launched his own line in 1957, after leaving his job at Dior, and had had great success with his selling point of 'tailoring with a twist'. Otherwise plain swing-coats came with exaggerated, oversized collars, pleated to remain rigid and cocoon the face; shift dresses were embossed with the ghostly shapes of lapels, prefiguring the sort of phantom detailing favoured by Rei Kawakubo and Martin Margiela more than thirty years later. Simple, sophisticated day dresses, coats and skirts were given new direction with unexpected swagging and draping of excess material at the hemline, lending a modern elegance to traditional pieces. Cardin's early designs, including bubble skirts, unstructured chemise dresses and panel-less coats, were a strong new take on minimal elegance, tempered by a nostalgia for the couture tradition within which he had been raised.

The general eagerness for progress, however, propelled Cardin and his contemporaries towards a more 'futuristic' vein. If luxury and a feminine silhouette were the established codes, then Cardin found inspiration in the most divergent extreme. He began creating pieces in new fabrics and materials that were not at all form-fitting, not elegant in the traditional sense, but shocking in their otherness and hard to categorize within existing fashion parlance. His excellence at tailoring remained crucial, but he began to use it to create severe, hard-angled garments, seeking to explore and test the limits of dimensions. The balloon dress of 1959, for example, seemed entirely devoid of structure until a drawstring cord was pulled and the entire garment wrapped itself around the wearer's body. Pioneering the use of new materials, including heavier wool, gaberdine and jersey rib, Cardin created pieces that would stand away from the body and produce a modern silhouette more in keeping with the extremes of the generation for which he found himself designing. 'More inventive, more beautifully coloured and textured than ever', declared *Vogue*. 'Double faced fabrics, twill, gabardine, crepe and cotton are particularly effective, firm and smooth, with plenty of body. They give a softly luxurious air to the most pared down lines.'[2]

Unlike Cristóbal Balenciaga, whose fluidity of form often referenced medievalism in its cowling and shrouding, or Paul Poiret, whose own rigidity of silhouette was imported from the East with allusions to the kimono, Cardin's outlines took geometry as a base. He was interested in the manipulation of shapes, particularly angular ones and those that had not been used to make clothing before. Circles, for instance, had been used previously in the cutting and manufacturing of skirts (with the body as centre, fanning outwards horizontally), but – as in the case of the balloon dress – Cardin turned them vertical, into a rectilinear pattern, and literally brought a new dimension to fashion.

Less is ... Modern

PIERRE CARDIN

1959: In the years after he left his post at Christian Dior, Cardin built on the tailoring skills he had learnt there to create minimalist, modern, sculptural suiting (right).

1959: Cardin's early couture (far right) was characterized by subtle and unexpected enhancement to forms, by enlarged, cocooning collars or draped, bagged-out hems.

1959: Traditional couture shapes were narrowed and simplified (below), excess was eliminated and seams were streamlined to create outerwear with a new sobriety of silhouette.

1959: At the end of the 1950s Cardin worked to eliminate excess from tailoring (below, right), with his boxy jackets, plain lapels and narrow, dart-less skirts.

1979: Cardin's pieces were bold and angular, but not heavily embellished, for a look that was functional but futuristic (right).

1963: Cardin's starting point was traditional tailoring, which he attempted to distil to its most functional level (right, bottom).

'My way was to draw something of the future,' Cardin said at his sixtieth anniversary celebration, 'to be young, to see that a woman could be free. I wanted to give women in the 1960s a chance to work, to sit, to take the car and drive in my dresses.'[3] Once again, female emancipation was the driving force behind a new movement in fashion, and how better to instigate that radical new vision than with a minimalist aesthetic and reductivist approach? Consumers were used to the simple styles of the post-war economy; they had also become familiar with a more pared-down version of elegance, thanks to Dior's New Look, and the fashion press were full of a futuristic sense of streamlining. According to *Vogue* in 1966,

Cheap labour with superior hand skills became very scarce and the little, uncluttered dress which we bought grudgingly at first out of necessity began to be appreciated for itself. Where simple clothes before this time had redeemed their lack of ornament by intricate and subtle cutting and

PIERRE CARDIN

Spring/Summer 1971: The only form of embellishment for many of the futurists complied with a code of function and ease; large pockets, collars and yokes were emphasized through colour and concept (right).

1970: Cardin's use of abstract geometry (far right) gave new, ergonomic dimensions to clothing – one reason he was thought of as such a forward-looking designer.

Spring/Summer 1971: The futurist designers of the 1960s and 1970s applied geometric concepts to clothing, hence these round-ended trousers and cosmonaut helmet (below).

1966: A white cocktail dress (below, right) shows some of Cardin's early experimental work with structure and form, as well as the beginning of his divergence from tradition.

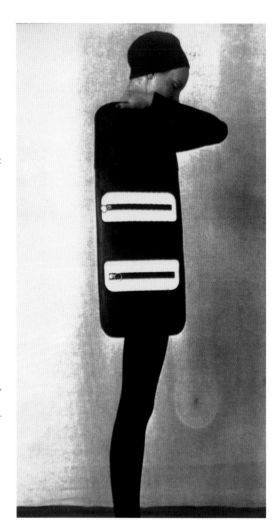

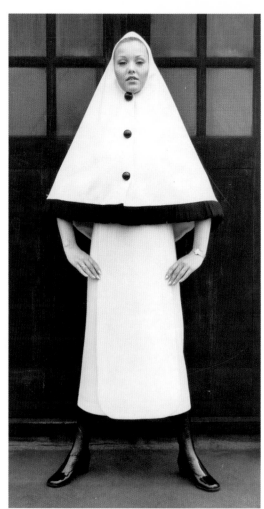

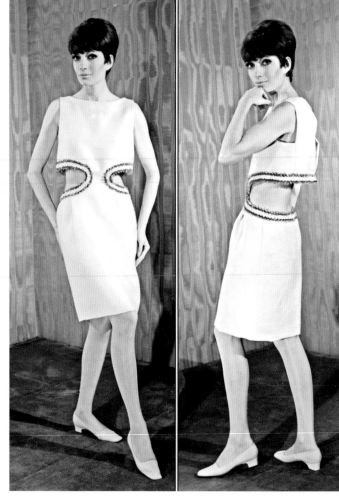

PIERRE CARDIN

1968: Simplified shapes (right) stood away from the body in Cardin's collections.

Autumn/Winter 1968–69: Cardin developed new materials and fabrics (below) to render precisely his vision of practical 'space-age fashion'.

1970: Such was the reputation of his functional aesthetic and uniform-led collections that Cardin designed a futuristic nurse's ensemble (below, right).

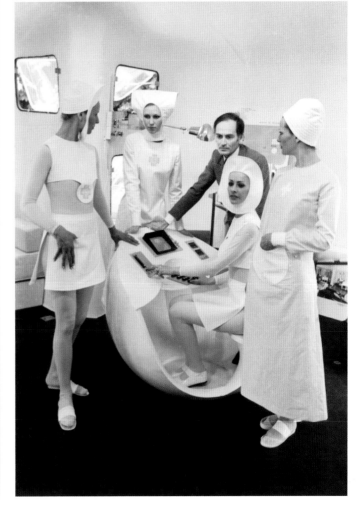

Less is … Modern

PIERRE CARDIN

1966: By extending his practical and pared-down design aesthetic to accessories and other aspects of modern life (right), Cardin purveyed a minimalist code for living.

Spring/Summer 1975: Cardin's draped pieces in wool crêpe were simple and chic (right, bottom), with slit pockets that did not bulk up or complicate the silhouette.

seaming, we now were asked to appreciate the two-seam dress, the A-line, the shift. It seemed that necessity was also the mother of the new aesthetic.[4]

Cardin's square-cut shift dresses allowed ultra-mobility and ease of movement, and the only adornment came in the form of cut-out panels or swirls, and scientifically de-sexualized anatomical detailing. Even when enhancing dresses with conical breasts and moulded panels, Cardin ensured that garments remained sterile and desensualized, thanks to thick opaque tights, sturdy thigh-high boots and the layering of dresses over ribbed bodysuits – all clinically cut, all clinically finished and all clinical in their determinedly futurist–utility aesthetic.

Cardin's 'Cosmos' collection of Spring/Summer 1964 was a landmark not only in his career but also in the social development of the 1960s. Its tunic and hose for men and women, its flat-cut and square-cut, hard-edged and undecorated, interchangeable garments characterized all that was forward-looking, open-minded and wilfully functional about the decade, and – despite being seen at first as somewhat outré – it paved the way for further experimentation. Cardin himself patented Cardine in 1968, a stiff and uncrushable technofabric (one of the first of its kind) that could be embossed with a pattern, and he also began to explore the use of plastics in clothing.

The 'Space Age' heralded a revolution within fashion, and it is interesting to note the importance of minimalism at this point: a spare, clean, sometimes severe line was seen as modishly futuristic. Excessive detail equated to the bourgeois fussiness of the previous generation. It was, in essence, the same revolution that Chanel had brought about in the 1920s, and it had at its heart the notion of an emancipated woman, whose clothes let her live in the style now available to her. The caption of a *Vogue* shoot in 1965 sums up the sense of wonder attached to the clothes made by the likes of Cardin and André Courrèges (born 1923): 'Cape Courrèges:

PIERRE CARDIN

1968: Short, well-proportioned dresses worn with thigh-high boots were key to Cardin's ergonomic look (right); the rigidity of the skirt is thanks to his patented material Cardine, which could be embossed with a three-dimensional pattern.

1972: Experimenting with geometric shapes and a new, more sculptural construction technique (far right), Cardin reworked the staples of the masculine and feminine wardrobes.

Autumn/Winter 1968–69: Cardin's space-age designs were characterized by a simple, streamlined look (bottom).

Less is ... Modern

ANDRÉ COURRÈGES

1967: Courrèges was among the first designers to advocate trousers for women (below), as a practical and more streamlined alternative to skirts and dresses.

1965: Actress Catherine Deneuve (bottom) in signature Courrèges square-cut coat and flat boots.

Jumping-off point. Click. Courrèges country. High Altitude. New proportions. Click. New fashion world. What next?'[5]

Courrèges's take on futuristic minimalism was similarly interested in reordering womenswear, but he was concerned less with making the extant feminine codes more comfortable and practical than with creating a female wardrobe that rivalled that of a man in terms of ease and simplicity. He was one of the first designers since Chanel – and there would be many more – to take inspiration from the pairing of separates as a modern mode of dressing. His aim was not to reassign aspects of menswear to women, but to provide women with a not-yet-conceived method of dressing. His designs were influenced by the severe angles and starkness of the times, playing with geometry and cut to achieve a look that was unrecognizable when compared with anything that had come before. 'The colour for new year is white, white, white', pronounced *Vogue*, after Cardin and Courrèges both showed monotonal collections. 'For the gentle spacegirl [there are] spare shoulders and a clinical collar, softened by a big sweep to the shoulder.'[6] Of course, every imagining of the future is tainted by its own timeliness, and these versions of projected 'spacewear' now seem clichéd and almost childlike.

Nevertheless, Courrèges spurned the prevailing 1950s archetype of the voluptuous woman with yards of skirts teetering atop a pair of high heels, and presented a new view of femininity for the new decade with his versions of female basics. Having first trained as a civil engineer, he was aware of practicality in a different way from Cardin, and he took inspiration from such architects as Le Corbusier, admiring the way in which they were able to pare buildings back to their essential functions while emphasizing the striking and brutal beauty that those functions could generate. While such modernizers as Chanel and Cardin saw a certain aesthetic value in simplified garments, there were others, such as Madeleine Vionnet, Balenciaga and

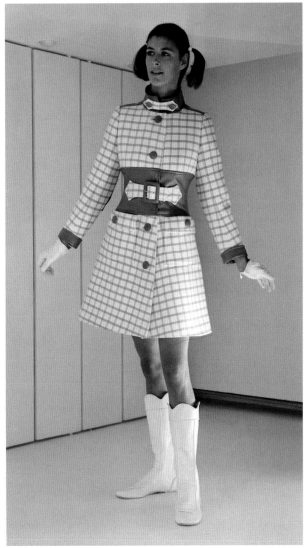

ANDRÉ COURRÈGES

Spring/Summer 1972: The trademarks of the space-age minimalists were practicality and comfort (above, left), combined with a sparseness that invoked a very time-specific idea of the future.

The eponymous 'Courrèges boot' (left) offered a practical alternative to the stiletto, and encouraged paring down as a way of life.

Autumn/Winter 1968–69: Working closely with geometric shapes and patterns (above), Courrèges pioneered a figure-conscious, fuller silhouette designed for the ultimate physical freedom for the wearer.

Less is ... Modern

ANDRÉ COURRÈGES

1969: During the 1960s, the tunic evolved into the minidress, picked out here (opposite, top) with body-conscious detailing and A-line shape to unencumber the wearer.

1969: Courrèges was concerned less with simplifying womenswear than with adapting menswear to feminine needs (opposite, bottom), hence his preoccupation with tailoring and suiting.

Courrèges (who founded his own house in 1961), who believed the most essential beauty to be present in that very simplification, and revelled in the attendant elegance of reductivism.

Rather than cutting around the body, Courrèges used his patterns to free it, creating A-line shift dresses that stood away from an uninhibited wearer, and focusing on the practicalities of each garment in itself as a foundation for a system of dressing. The dress he found to be either too cumbersome or too restrictive, so he concentrated on a tunic, which could been worn with thick, modesty-preserving tights or with trousers. In his quest for functionalism, Courrèges is credited with having invented the miniskirt, but we have seen that the tunic in its many guises – from Poiret's lampshade version via Balenciaga's luxurious 'sacque' dresses – had previously been integral to the evolution of minimalist design. Undoubtedly Courrèges was drawn to the fact that it is a formative garment with a dual function, and it became a staple piece in his collections. He also broke the prevalent trend of women wearing skirts, featuring trousers in many of his collections out of necessity, since they provided the clean, streamlined look he always had in mind.

Courrèges also denounced the stiletto as playing a key role in the subordination of women, and created his eponymous boot, a flat-soled, sporty-looking shoe made from white kid, calf or patent leather with slots around the top and often a small bow or tassel at the front. It marked the instigation of the reductivist lifestyle: Courrèges was one of the first designers to encourage minimalism (or, at least, paring down) as a way of life, providing the means to apply it beyond mere fashion. He also showed his collections on models who were accessorized with space-age helmets and bonnets, as if to imply – as did Cardin, with his sci-fi spectacles and Op Art vinyl gloves – that the new aesthetic was destined to be all-pervasive, that the future was a way of life that would soon encompass all others. 'I represented the need of the century', he said in 1986.[7]

Museums the world over hold pieces by Courrèges and Cardin that have not aged well because of the synthetic nature of their make-up; the early plastics and acetates used are unable to withstand mould and rot. Much discussion has focused latterly on the 1960s designers as commercially innovative, with their never-ending patents and franchising (to this day, Cardin lends his name to a type of Japanese alarm clock), but creatively rather naïve or lacklustre – half-baked, even. There can be no doubt that, with informed hindsight, some of the futurists' designs are comical – such are the perils of retro-futurism – but sophistication of technique and complexity of design are evident in much of Courrèges's work.

Indeed, Courrèges's pieces were copied internationally and almost instantaneously (to the extent that he renounced the catwalk and worked only with private customers), but these copies had none of the finesse or architecture of the originals. The intricacy of construction can be seen in the chevron stitching Courrèges liked to use on pockets, to make them sturdier but also to flatten the line at which they were attached to the body of the garment; similarly, he was inventive with those parts of clothing that seemed generic or standard, using bib yokes and keyhole necklines, as well as patch pockets. Any surface embellishment pointed to the construction and therefore the functionality of the piece: stitching came in contrasting colours to the fabric to emphasize the engineering of the garment, while adornment was minor (belts on coats and jackets reached only halfway around the back) and welted seams (those strengthened with the fabric overlaid and then top-stitched) served a quietly decorative purpose.

Fashion Meets Art: Yves Saint Laurent

If Courrèges was the architect of future fashion, then the up-and-coming Saint Laurent (1936–2008) was the artist. As chief designer at Dior he had successfully launched the 'trapeze line' in 1958, a collection of trapezoid shifts in perfect harmony not only with Balenciaga's final collections but also with the new directions of Cardin and Courrèges. The dresses heralded a new lease of life – not to mention a new height of hemline – for daywear. Saint Laurent's collection of 1960 for Dior, however, was more problematic; it was inspired by the bohemian Left Bank look, and featured knitted polo necks with leather jackets, crocodile jackets with fur collars and a fur coat with knitted sleeves, all in sombre colours, all separates. Obviously, Saint Laurent's foresight was immense, but those in charge of the label felt he had taken a rather deviant and divergent, non-commercial route. Dior at that time accounted for almost half of France's fashion exports, and, when Saint Laurent returned from his military service in Algeria, he found Marc Bohan at its helm instead.

On opening his own house in 1962, Saint Laurent continued to champion in his collections that which he felt was culturally apposite and socially important, from the Left Bank beatniks to the student protesters of 1968, to whom he dedicated a collection of tailored trousers. His sympathies lay with youthful rebels, and he used his designs to reflect this, creating pieces inspired by timeless, chic classics but reinventing them in daring new ways. The trouser suit and Le Smoking, of course, were his best-known achievements, but the sheer blouse and safari suit and the trench coat belted over trousers were also iconic looks. His foray into minimalism was fleeting, but it was to become one of the most conspicuous and recognizable examples of the meeting between the burgeoning art movement and the fashion theme of the same

Less is ... Modern

YVES SAINT LAURENT

1968: Just as the American sportswear designers had given women a new everyday uniform, Saint Laurent's tailoring added further expression and practicality to womenswear.

name. It was, in fact, one of the first true marriages of fashion and art.

'Geometry is a favourite of the couture this season', declared *Vogue* in September 1965. 'Geometric seams and shapes are to be seen at Saint Laurent ... with short jersey shifts, newly proportioned in clear blocks and bold lines of colour. In a collection where every dress was strikingly young, this was his youngest dress shape: small, high-waisted, supple and two-coloured.'[8] The garment in question was the now-famous Mondrian dress. Although it mirrored Cardin's square-cut tunics, it was slightly longer, so remained firmly in the category of respectable daywear, with no need for opaque tights, bodysuits or ergonomic trousers, as so many of Courrèges's shifts demanded. Saint Laurent pioneered minimalism not for the future's sake but for the present, with elegantly streamlined garments that would slide easily into any wardrobe or social occasion, while making a strong, directional statement. In doing so, he was one of the first designers to realize the graphic potential of each plane of a dress. What better surface on which to express Piet Mondrian's ideas of geometric abstraction and universality of concept than the flat, uncluttered lines of a shift dress?

The artist in question belonged to the De Stijl movement, a Dutch school founded in 1917 that sought to express absolute purity and essence in as simple a way as possible. The movement was an offshoot of Bauhaus, which advocated logic and harmony in clean lines and asymmetry, angles, geometric shapes and block colours. De Stijl artists created paintings, but also influenced furniture and architecture. It was, again, a lifestyle choice, something similar to the futuristic scenarios proposed by Cardin and Courrèges, in which a single aesthetic would be the driving force behind design, and in which everything was sterile, angular and ergonomic. By the late 1960s, Cardin was designing nurses' uniforms in that vein, following on from his all-white 'Cosmos' collection; he began working on

furniture, too, and even created a private jet, decorated inside and out with his signature stripes.

Saint Laurent's Mondrian collection of shift dresses not only successfully validated the De Stijl movement's notion of design for life, by showing it to be both practical and aesthetically pleasing, but also proved that simple design was not always the easiest to achieve. The intricacy of the garment is belied by its naïve graphic: each structural and shaping seam is concealed in the grid of rectangles; each block of colour is a separately inserted panel of jersey; the body is carefully accommodated in a way that compromises neither the angular visual scheme of the garment nor the practical ease and mobility of the wearer. In yet another 'first' for the futurists, Saint Laurent had created the body as a living piece of art, in a feat of virtuosity not seen since Elsa Schiaparelli's Surrealist tributes of the 1930s, when the artist collaborated with Jean Cocteau, Salvador Dalí and Alberto Giacometti, among others.

The Mondrian pieces are, perhaps, the first official instance of minimalism in fashion. What we have seen prior to this was a pragmatic paring-down of clothing for social, cultural and practical reasons; here, the notion was first and foremost to create a conceptual piece that tallied with the tenets of an art movement. Although the impetuses are not dissimilar, this introduction of concept – beyond construction or commerce – is an important stage in the development of minimalism in fashion, and it remains a dividing line that can be used to separate the various interpretations of reductivist style. While many designers are happy to admit that they see their work as crossing over into the territory of art, others are not, because they see fashion as something vital and alive, whereas art cannot be inhabited in the same way. None of this debate would be possible if Saint Laurent had not experimented with Mondrian's graphics.

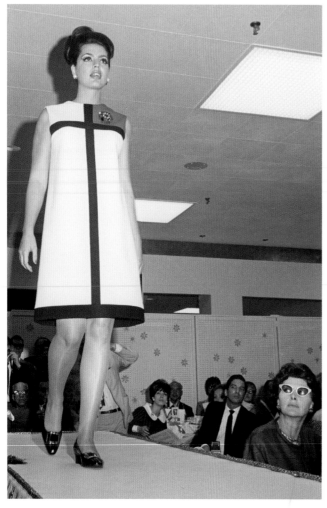

The New Nostalgia

As the 1960s drew to a close, there began an overall softening of line and silhouette that would take hold in the 1970s. Courrèges attempted a return to the public consciousness with a ready-to-wear collection called 'Couture Future', which he launched in 1969. It lacked none of the designer's signature style, with A-line structured shifts and welted-seam coats, but what had been seminal at the outset of the decade now looked a little passé. The pendulum had reversed, just as it had after the Second World War, when whimsical, feminine pieces came to the fore. There had been a sense then that Brutalism and severity were closely allied to Hitler and to the totalitarian absolutism that had been defeated; at the end of the 1960s – with the Vietnam conflict at its height, provoking a countercultural nostalgia for the peaceful and the pastoral – the angularity of minimalism once more became unpopular.

It was to remain thus for almost a decade, although such notable designers as Jean Muir (1928–1995) under the label Jane & Jane continued to work according to an unadorned aesthetic. Muir's soft jersey and chunky knits remained acceptably modish because, although very simple, they retained something of the Arts and Crafts movement and felt suitably rustic, for all their creator's mathematical and technical expertise. Muir was similar to Vionnet and Claire McCardell in her quest for clothes that felt right on the body and were equipped to move with the wearer, and, in order to ensure that, she created toiles (test garments, used to check patterns) against her own body. It produces a strange juxtaposition to place her in the same category as Saint Laurent, but she was the natural progression from the hard-edged look of the 1960s.

Feelings were similar in the United States, where the hippy movement had taken a much stronger hold than it had in Europe. By the end of the 1970s, fashion was ready to calm down once more, but consumers were keen to retain the

Less is ... Modern

ZORAN

1982: Architect-turned-designer Zoran Ladicorbic commercialized minimalism as a luxury aesthetic with his plain cashmere separates and range of basics.

freedom and comfort of that decade. It was this fusion of comfort and cool – once more, Chanel's classic formula of quiet and pragmatic style – that gave rise to one of the design phenomena of the late 1970s: Zoran Ladicorbic (born 1947), a Yugoslavian architect based in New York.

After a career in retail, Zoran (as both he and his label came to be known) created his first collection in 1976, using only the finest fabrics available. Staple materials and Zoran signatures included cashmere, silk, velvet and high-quality wool, all used to sculpt elegant and basic pieces that whispered of luxury, rather than shouting about it. Zoran's ethic was discreet quality, with careful attention paid to the cut and finish of garments; these were as important, in his eyes, as surface embellishment. 'Each item has the cleanest possible outline: from the slashed neck cashmere jersey – its edges apparently unfinished – to the layering of a grey flannel suit, utterly plain and soft, over a shimmering vest. Zoran's skirts are straight and unconstricting, his jackets free from collars, cuffs and buttons, his dresses mere slips: everything is interchangeable, nothing is obtrusive', said *Vogue*.[9]

It was the perfect aesthetic for the era: casual and restrained, in a muted palette of white, cream, grey and nude. Zoran had a very specific clientele, which included Candice Bergen, Lauren Hutton and Isabella Rossellini. 'A certain woman has impressed herself on Zoran's mind', continued *Vogue*. 'She is mature and educated and allows herself a sizable budget for clothes. She travels fast, works hard and enjoys a sophisticated lifestyle.'[10] Zoran's clothes were timeless and trendless, allowing the wearer to blend into any situation. Traditionally, buyers came to his studio, a vast space empty but for a few garments hanging from scaffolding in a corner, and would pick out their wardrobe for the next year. 'A true devotee ... will pay a couple of visits a year, and spend several thousand dollars on an entire wardrobe', he told *Vogue* in 1983.[11]

ZORAN

1983: Zoran's separates
came in a toned-down
palette of neutrals to create
a capsule of interchangeable,
minimalist pieces.

Zoran was on the cusp of truly modern fashion: he handled customers and clothing in a way not dissimilar to that of such designers as Balenciaga and Vionnet – personally and in a quiet salon – yet his clothes were not couture. They were crafted lovingly, but they were not complex and they were not statement pieces. His entire operation was also suffused with the sort of overriding concept that became popular and widespread only with the rise of the Japanese designers later in the 1980s. Zoran's workspace, definitive and indicative of his aesthetic; his signatures, imbued with the geometry and vision of his years as an architect; his clothes, part of an entire lifestyle informed by minimalism: such a standpoint at this moment was decidedly anti-fashion.

Notes

1 'Lean and Easy', *Vogue* (UK), January 1962, p. 18.
2 'Key Points in Paris', *Vogue* (UK), March 1966, p. 105.
3 Quoted in Suzy Menkes, 'Pierre Cardin: One Step Ahead of Tomorrow', *International Herald Tribune*, 22 March 2010.
4 'What Next in Vogue', *Vogue* (UK), October 1966, p. 158.
5 'Cape Courrèges', photographs by David Bailey, *Vogue* (UK), March 1965, p. 109.
6 'Young Idea Say It's Never Seen White Like This Before', *Vogue* (UK), January 1966, p. 61.
7 Quoted in Michael Gross, 'Courrèges: New Venture, Old Optimism', *New York Times*, 17 January 1986, p. 18.
8 'Paris: The New Jersey Geometry', *Vogue* (UK), September 1965, p. 96.
9 'Design for Living', *Vogue* (UK), March 1983, p. 178.
10 *Ibid*.
11 *Ibid*.

Less is ... Different

Minimalism as Counterculture, 1978–88

YOHJI YAMAMOTO

Autumn/Winter 1989–90: Yamamoto's flat-cut garments brought a new sense of dimension to fashion, considering the wearer's body in the round rather than from head to toe, and featuring asymmetrical cut-outs and add-ons.

'If there are, say, ten great designers in the world right now, then at least three of them are Japanese', declared a special issue of *Time* magazine in 1983. 'These are not international celebrity couturiers, doing cunning variations on conventional forms. These are revolutionaries, insurgents whose aim is to modify ... the shape and form of clothing itself.'[1]

In the wake of 1970s liberalism – particularly as the hippy movement ended and punk came to the fore – the world of high fashion took an even more pronounced *haute bourgeois* direction. Designers Guy Paulin (1945–1990) and Marc Bohan (born 1926), who succeeded Saint Laurent as creative director at the house of Dior, continued to create superbly *bon chic, bon genre* suiting and separates with a reductivist and streamlined aesthetic, but there was something undeniably grown-up about them. There was all the restrained and practical modern elegance of early Chanel, with none of the shock value or progressive elements.

That is not to discredit Bohan, whose twenty-nine-year tenure as head of Dior was a fluent and successful one. 'N'oubliez pas la femme', he told *Vogue* in 1963, and, in common with that of Chanel, his work was primarily informed by the female body and the feminine existence.[2] He understood that elegance and practicality need not, and should not, be mutually exclusive in modern life. His work during the 1960s could be either opulent and embellished – such as the embroidered gold tulle gown he created for Spring/Summer 1964 – or quietly refined, as were his gazar cocktail dresses and lambswool swing coats, which show a simplicity and structuralism not unlike that of Cristóbal Balenciaga. Adornment for Bohan came in discreet and functional doses: a small bow defines the waist; a grosgrain tie at the shoulder marks the origin of a gown's line and drop. The important balance was between decoration and self-consciousness; anything added must not make the garment less easy to wear.

Bohan's period of assisting the great couturier Edward Molyneux gave him a grounding in clean and functional pattern-cutting, not to mention an appreciation of luxurious fabrics, both of which came together in his collections for Dior to produce clothes that were stark in cut but sumptuous in colour and texture. It was in tailoring that he progressed furthest, regularly producing suits, jackets and shifts with directional shapes and lines that influenced others for seasons to come. Yet the pieces were timeless, born of careful avoidance of 'over-stepping the boundaries of classicism' (as he told an interiors magazine in 1994),[3] which meant they were commercially very successful among the ritzier levels of European and American society.

But there were uneasy undercurrents in fashion at this point. At the start of the decade fashion attempted to consolidate what it had learnt in the 1960s and unlearnt in the 1970s: the process of designing for and catering to a youthful mass market. Chanel and Yves Saint Laurent had proved that there was a certain adventurous aspect of minimalism, combining the progressive with the pragmatic, and had therefore appealed to a certain rather knowing sect of fashionable society. By default, their customers were often younger and more spirited, eager for change both socially and sartorially. The early 1980s were, of course, a confused confluence of various social pressures – recession, redundancies, reform and socio-sexual revolution – which slowed and then gradually rebooted the global economy.

Avant-garde Minimalism: Miyake, Yamamoto and Kawakubo

Minimalist fashion had already proved its ability to make political and social statements, and what better way to stand out from the crowd during the 1980s, with life about to reach its most urbane and commercially excessive since the Edwardian era, than by shunning the received

twinsets, tailoring and bourgeois style? With the arrival of Japanese designers Issey Miyake, Yohji Yamamoto and Rei Kawakubo, there came once more a surge of youth culture that invigorated fashion from the outside, from designers beyond the establishment who sought to reimagine established concepts of clothing. And, once more, they concerned themselves with purity of design, with functionality, and with minimalism.

Miyake (born 1938) was perhaps buoyed less than his compatriot designers by the youth market, but he and his clothes nevertheless represented a conscious alliance with the avant-garde and openly intellectual. His pieces were challenging in a way that those by Bohan and even to some extent Saint Laurent no longer were, despite their being unmistakably two of the finest designers and couturiers of the age. Saint Laurent had shocked with his tuxedos, sheer blouses and safari suits, but it was Miyake who startled the next generation.

Arriving on the international scene in the early 1970s, shortly after Kenzo Takada (born 1939) had stormed Paris with his imaginative fusion of Eastern design and Western decoration, Miyake was a key player in a wave of new orientalism. This was not the bird-printed, bejewelled and heavily embroidered kimonos that Paul Poiret had adapted into a sumptuous early twentieth-century chinoiserie; it was, in fact, something more like his Confucius coat, which was received so badly by the Princess Bariatinsky. The new wave represented a similarly groundbreaking alignment of Western fashion with those qualities of Eastern clothing that make for ease of movement and a spare and stark, but impressive and dignified, appearance.

Miyake is often known as an architect of fabric, for his ability to manipulate cloth into complex structures that cocoon the body, and form radically different shapes according to the wearer. His signature concept is 'A Piece of Cloth', after which he named the A-POC diffusion line in 1997, which highlights the flat cut so common

CHRISTIAN DIOR
BY MARC BOHAN

1965: After the death of Dior, the house continued with its idiosyncratically exuberant and architectural but feminine version of minimalism (opposite, top), but the look became increasingly bourgeois as fashion took a less high-gloss direction.

GUY PAULIN

Such chic Parisian designers as Guy Paulin made clothing that was fuss-free and streamlined (opposite, bottom) but essentially bourgeois and mainstream.

ISSEY MIYAKE

Ensemble *c.* 1978 (right, top); waistcoat from Autumn/Winter 1983–84 (right): Miyake worked with unexpected fabrics and the sorts of silhouettes found more often in traditional Japanese workwear.

Less is ... Different

ISSEY MIYAKE

1997: The cut-out
guidelines from Miyake's
ingenious A-POC collection
(right), in which the
customer creates their
own garment from a single
piece of material.

Autumn/Winter 1984–85:
Miyake's clothes (right,
bottom) are body-
conscious by being
anthropologically
considered and riffing on
the body of the wearer.

Spring/Summer 1989:
Moulded and pleated
clothing explores the space
around the wearer as well as
the space within the pieces;
Miyake's main concern is the
ma, the space between the
wearer and their garments.

in Japanese design. The logic is that covering a body with a single piece of cloth creates a space (*ma*) between it and the body of the wearer that equates to a natural freedom. This space varies with each body, of course, creating a piece of clothing that is unique on each person.

Compared to the breakthroughs in production with which such designers as Claire McCardell are credited – that is, garments made from several cut pieces and panels, designed to fit uniformly on each customer – Miyake's work seemed to be driving directly against the future, which lay in mass markets and mass production. Such ideas were unheard of in Western fashion. The only designer to whom he would appear to have any similarity is Mariano Fortuny, who was equally uninterested in the complexities of cut and pattern, but driven mainly by the form and function of his pieces on the body.

But Miyake has made it a personal goal to explore the very furthest possibilities of cloth. He is nothing if not an innovator, whereas Fortuny was happy to find a medium that suited his aesthetic and continue without development. Miyake's use of cutting-edge fabrics – such as reinforced polyester, nylon and newly developed technofabrics – means his pieces seemingly possess totally different elemental properties from anything else that came before them. He combines computer technology with traditional cutting, knitting and sewing techniques to form clothes that are uniquely bonded, uniquely fused, unique in their creation and unique upon the body. 'I feel that I have found a new way to give individuality to today's mass-produced clothing', he said in 2009.[4]

After his Paris debut in 1973, Miyake quickly developed a cult following of directional and avant-garde customers, but he also swayed the prevailing aesthetic of the time. Complex and detailed though his concepts and inspirations often were, his clothes were defiantly easy to wear and easy to live in. At a time when the hallowed institution of haute couture was crumbling in the face of a broader ready-to-wear movement, he

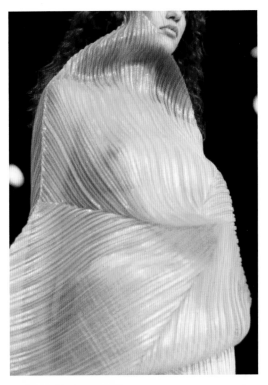

Less is ... Different

Dress by Yohji Yamamoto (1983); trousers by Comme des Garçons (c. 1985): The Japanese designers rebelled against Western fashion conceits and created a new aesthetic that carried all before it.

brought a new sort of couture to the fore, one that placed no less emphasis on craftsmanship, manpower, virtuosity and elegance, but which celebrated each in its simplest and most functional format. No longer were thousands of painstaking (and expensive) hours spent embroidering, cutting or measuring. Instead, there was new technology and yet another 'new look'.

Miyake's silhouette is tricky to define, because it has altered so many times, but one of its idiosyncrasies is its flat, kimono-style cut. Another is its body-consciousness, not that of the bandage dresses and clinging pieces designed in the mid-1980s by Hervé Léger and Azzedine Alaïa, for example, but in the truer, anthropological sense of moulding and riffing on the wearer's own form, whether it be by revealing or concealing the body. Signature Miyake pieces include bodysuits and tights, often decorated with a tattooed body pattern. Such pieces as the red plastic bodice from his Autumn/Winter 1980–81 collection, with its moulded nipples and navel, are more obviously body-con in the traditional sense, whereas the thinking behind the free-sized 'A-POC' line is rather more progressive: the garments are sold as a knit tube, which the wearer then customizes and cuts shapes from, creating exactly what she wants in exactly the fit she wants. If minimalism is characterized by the non-prescription of form and the descriptivism of function, then Miyake's work comes very close to its essence.

Miyake's clothes are also characterized by transformation, a recurring feature among the Japanese minimalists, in yet another attempt to fuse the geometries of clothing with the exigencies of modern living. His knit square of 1976 had the capacity to become a coat and matching bikini; he creates capes that slip from the shoulders and form skirts, and enveloping hoods that can also act as sleeves or collars. Much of his *oeuvre* is created with the intent that its shape can be fluidly defined by its compression and extension. In that respect, Miyake owes much to the likes of Fortuny and Madeleine Vionnet (his self-proclaimed greatest

influence), which fact underpins a certain historical dimension in his work. Minimalism is often categorized as 'future clothing', its sleek, streamlined and often severe lines taken as a sign of scientific exploration and a stripping down that does away with the human story of dress, but historicism does play an important part in the movement. Not since Vionnet has a designer worked so closely with the geometries and complexities of cloth as Miyake, with his draping and folding on the bias, and his attention to clothing in its dynamism, rather than when static.

Miyake's style is reminiscent, too, of the dancers and would-be natural dressers who had turned to Fortuny more than sixty years earlier. Indeed, Miyake's first pleated collection, for Autumn/Winter 1989–90, mirrored the Venetian designer's Delphos dress very closely. Instead of silk, though, Miyake chose to work in a typically modern fabric: a type of polyester/silk mix cut to shape by ultrasonic waves. But, where standard practice is to pleat fabric before it is cut to pattern and sewn together in panels (as Fortuny did), Miyake's pleating process comes after the garment has been assembled, creating a rough feel to the pleats and giving them the agency to change physically and to manipulate the shape of the final garment, which in turn is shaped anew by every different wearer. In 1993, after the success of this collection, he established a second line, 'Pleats Please', to focus on developing these pieces.

Yet, despite his experimentation and innovation, Miyake's work also concentrates on the rustic and basic, using the traditional heavy-woven, quilted *sashiko* cotton of rural workers' clothes, and he once turned a traditional farmer's backpack into a knitted jacket. 'I was trying to peel away to the limit of fashion', he explains.[5] It is this juxtaposition (or retro-futurism, as it may be described in certain instances) that lies at the heart of much minimalist design, a sense of nostalgia, perhaps, and certainly a sense of returning to a simpler idyll. Minimalists

Less is ... Different

are nostalgics with vision: they use modern technology to reach for the comfort of the past.

The work of Yohji Yamamoto (born 1943), for instance, harks back to ancient Japanese dress codes, and seeks to fuse them with elements of historic Western costume to create a perfect balancing of the simple and the sartorially aware. Lightweight, flat-cut crinoline skirts are worn with paper-soled brogues, or 'peasant shoes' as they are known, inspired by the footwear of Japanese workers. Luxurious coats and dresses are made from an acreage of fabric to which such workers would never have had access, but are cut and constructed in the way their clothes were. Such fusion represents a luxury that is often inherent in minimalism, but also highlights its potential for controversy. And it was for both that Yamamoto became known, alongside his good friend and fellow designer Rei Kawakubo (born 1942).

Both designers were part of the Tokyo Collection Office, a collective of fourteen young designers who were invited by the Chambre Syndicale de la Haute Couture (a sort of trade union for couturiers) to show in Paris in 1982, an indication of how much ground the Parisian Fédération de la Couture was willing to give in uncertain economic times. 'The Japanese have stormed Paris with difficult but certainly innovative clothes precisely when many Europeans, seemingly scared by recession, have turned super-conservative', blared the Canadian *Globe and Mail* in 1983.[6] The collections shown that season by Yamamoto and Kawakubo (who designs under the label Comme des Garçons) were anything but conservative: they worked mainly in black, often ripping and tearing holes in garments; bunching and layering fabric to such an extent that the body beneath was all but obscured; and showing their collections on pale models with no make-up, flat shoes and bruises painted on to their faces. They appealed to a younger market, who felt that Japan was a country heralding the future, but commentary on the shows and the subsequent press each

designer received were overwhelmingly backward-looking. Their aesthetic was dubbed 'Hiroshima chic', and general opinion held that it was negative, cynical and tasteless, not to mention unflattering and downright unfashionable.

This was a style press more used to the creations of Bohan, who never denied his attachment to the female form, nor his respect for classicism and sophistication. 'Japan has challenged the sexist concept that dress must be based on the shape of the body', wrote Suzy Menkes in 1986. 'An emphasis on fabric rather than form has set in motion a fashion revolution.'[7] That fashion revolution dealt in minimalism: the grandest gesture one could make at that time was to dress in a way that was as pared down as possible, stripped back and sometimes violently so. The term 'anti-fashion' came to be used to denote those who wore the dark clothes of the Japanese designers, brief and brutal in their lack of any discernible adornment but luxurious and opulent in their use of fabric and intricacy of cut. By ignoring Western trends and creating a collection of ostentatiously non-directional clothes, Yamamoto in turn began to influence Western trends, apparently in spite of himself.

One of the main tenets of the anti-fashion movement was similar to the ideology of Miyake: that clothes should reflect the wearer more than they should do any current trend. His penchant for the very architecture and essential foundations of clothing is something by which Yamamoto continued to be inspired, with an approach to clothing that drew similarly on a philosophical conceptualization. He saw clothes as a shelter for the body and spirit, and, as such, he thought there should be an interaction between the body and the garment. In common with Miyake, he felt the way to attempt this was to combine elements of Western fashion with the structure and theory of Japanese indigenous dress.

Having worked as a dressmaker in Tokyo making 'very form-fitting, terrible clothes for

Less is ... Different

women whose money came from their husbands or boyfriends',[8] Yamamoto set up his own label in 1972, and concentrated on formlessness from the outset. He worked largely in black, draping and layering the body in sombre and unstructured garments that refused to acknowledge the standard parts (hips, bottom and breasts) enhanced by Western clothing. This became known by the style press as the 'Jap wrap'. Pieces were kimono-esque in their resultant shape and androgynous look, and while many believed them to display a rather negative sort of stubbornness or intransigent need to shock, Yamamoto was actually exploring another facet of traditional Japanese aesthetics: the belief that limiting the use of colour and manipulation of garments was a means of achieving beauty.

Yamamoto also followed the Japanese convention of constructing clothing in the round, rather than the Western tradition of working from the neck down. This explains his fascination with asymmetry, unexpected flaps and extra pockets, all of which can be better appreciated in the dimensions in which he worked, rather than on paper as a sketch. The clothes are flat-cut but never flat-looking, again whispering of the interaction he hopes that the wearer has with their garment. Indeed, each piece has a label with the motto 'There is nothing so boring as a neat and tidy look', and Yamamoto sets great store by the importance of texture in his clothing, producing intentionally (and wittily) wrinkled collars and cuffs, crumpled outer layers and unfinished, trailing hems.

Kawakubo took this look to even further extremes at Comme des Garçons, and it was characterized in the press as 'la mode destroy'. Working with textile designer Hiroshi Matsushita, Kawakubo developed a system of 'loom-distressed weaves' for woollen jumpers and dresses that looked as though they were constituted more by holes than by knit. The lace-like, ripped effect contributed further to the idea of 'Hiroshima chic', and led many to

categorize her work as a 'bag lady' aesthetic. Kawakubo also came under attack in her home country, where – although the label was popular among the younger, more avant-garde crowd – those who wore her clothes were known as 'the crows' and often subjected to taunts in the street for their outré garb.

The deconstructivist take on fashion that Yamamoto and Kawakubo brought to Europe in the 1980s was as concerned with pulling apart yarns and knits as it was with pulling apart contemporary bourgeois notions of Western elegance. Their work in black and white was a means of configuring absence, rather than presence; the unstructured, wrapped look was an important experimentation with clothes that take shape from the very cloth with which they are constructed, rather than from the person inside them or even the designer who creates them. There was a sense of benign negation, but not necessarily one of negativity.

This negation is crucial to minimalism, which seeks not to suppress the wearer or their identity, but to reduce everything to an essential level, in order that existence might be simpler. It is the same ethic that was behind Chanel's take on womenswear, and the rise of American sportswear in the 1930s and 1940s. It would be behind Donna Karan's label, which she opened in 1985, as well as those of Giorgio Armani and Jil Sander.

There are those who would call Comme des Garçons conceptual rather than minimalist. Indeed, where deconstruction for Kawakubo reached the point of adding extra sleeves to garments and jacket detailing on to the backs of sweaters and trousers, swaddling models in vast amounts of wool and tulle, and creating artificial humps and lumps about the body, it cannot of course necessarily be called a paring down per se. The effect is hyperbolic, and that is not what one would expect of a minimalist. But the result, more broadly, was a stripping away of aesthetic. Kawakubo's continued and defiantly reductivist take on fashion, female beauty and

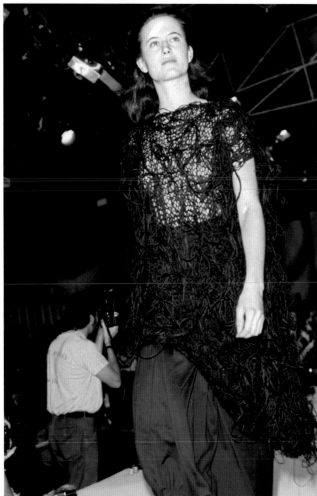

COMME DES GARÇONS

Autumn/Winter 1984–85:
Kawakubo's fascination with
black (top left) characterized
her early shows, which were
labelled 'Hiroshima chic' by
the style press.

Autumn/Winter 1984–85:
The emerging Japanese
designers became known for
their baggy and haphazard
layering of coarse, distressed
fabrics (top right).

Autumn/Winter 1984–85:
Kawakubo worked with dark
colours (bottom left) and
dramatic dishevelment,
pairing deliberately
unravelling knits with
long, austere skirts.

Autumn/Winter 1987–88:
Key aspects of Kawakubo's
collections (bottom right)
include asymmetry, layering
and a resolute avoidance of
a body-conscious silhouette.

the zeitgeist means that her influence on trends has always been informed by minimalism. The formlessness; the absolute imperative against conventional 'sexiness'; the attention to the vagaries of cloth and fabric rather than to the body; the monochrome palette; and, in particular, the unrelenting use of black: all these cast Kawakubo as a minimalist designer, albeit one of the most visionary.

'She wanted a shape that was not really a shape and yet was a shape', Kawakubo's translator told interviewers in 1984. 'She wondered if, of two layers, the proportions on one side and on the reverse side were different, what sort of effect that would have. It would probably have a very shapeless shape.'[9] Kawakubo's interests lie in fusing the traditional Japanese workwear aesthetic, in its essential simplicity, with the purism and starkness of modern architecture, as seen in buildings designed by Le Corbusier and Tadao Ando. This fusion finds meaning in the off-body silhouette of the kimono, which is stiffened in some places and body-skimming in others (although never revealing or clinging), and the various wrappings, layerings and formations it requires as a mode of dress. Comme des Garçons garments are often complex in their construction, but they are always unstructured and sober when worn, and this appealed to clients who were tiring of the *haute bourgeois* look that was so prevalent elsewhere. 'Sales of Comme des Garçons totalled ¥5.3 billion last year,' announced the *Japan Economic Journal* in 1982, 'up 30 per cent from 1980. Its sales at the exhibition in Paris last spring alone amounted to as much as some ¥100 million.'[10]

By the mid-1980s the Japanese influence on European and, more broadly, Western fashion was undeniable. Japanese designers had reached to the core of the Chambre Syndicale; they had awoken – and often scandalized – press and buyers with their brutalist creations and catwalk shows; they had provided an alternative to the glitz and glamour of the decade, and this

alternative was seized upon by the avant-garde. It was, then, only a matter of time before the pared-down and severe aesthetic made its way into mainstream collections and more commercial territory.

Notes

1 Jay Cocks, 'Into the Soul of Fabric: Japanese Designers Shape a Fashion Revolution in the West', *Time*, August 1983, p. 72.
2 Quoted in *Contemporary Fashion*, ed. Taryn Benbow-Pfalzgraf, Detroit (St James Press) 2002, p. 81.
3 Quoted in *Contemporary Fashion*, p. 81.
4 Quoted in Bonnie English, *Fashion: The Fifty Most Influential Designers in the World*, London (A & C Black) 2009, p. 104.
5 Quoted in Cocks, 'Into the Soul of Fabric'.
6 Joyce Carter, 'A New Wave from Japan', *Globe and Mail* (Canada), 10 May 1983.
7 Suzy Menkes, 'A Special Report on Japan: Forward with Fabrics', *The Times* (London), 11 July 1986.
8 Quoted in Cocks, 'Into the Soul of Fabric'.
9 Quoted in David Livingstone, 'Seeing Kawakubo', *Globe and Mail* (Canada), 20 November 1984.
10 'Young Fashion Designers Attract World Attention', *Japan Economic Journal*, 13 July 1982, p. 18.

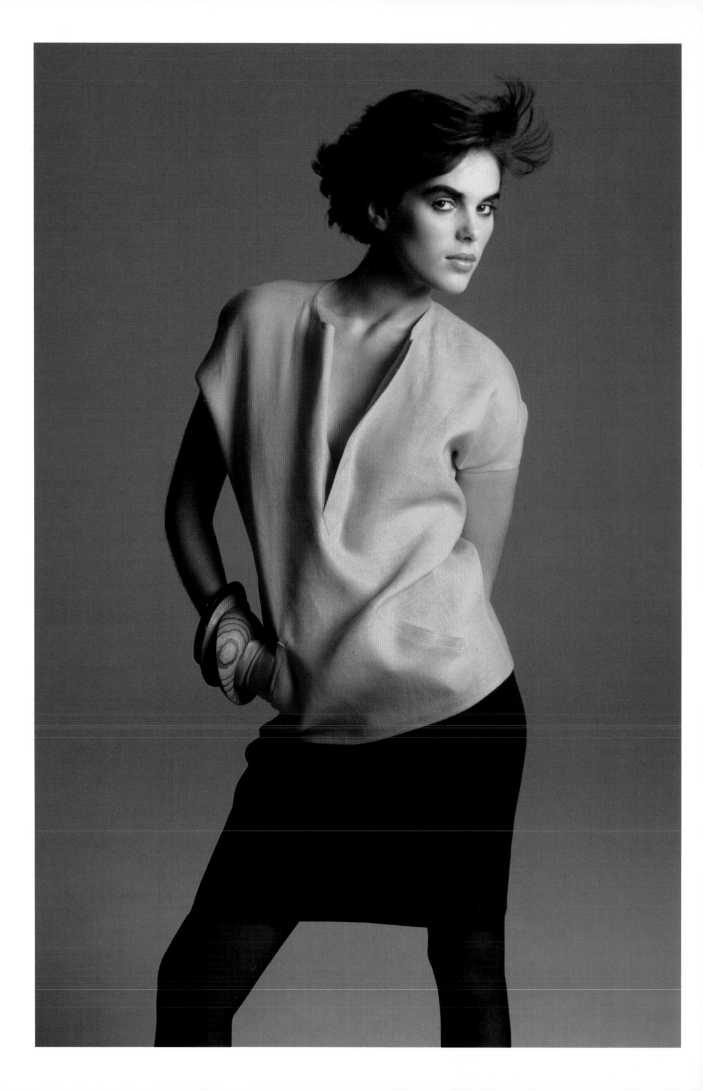

Less is ... Pure

The Designer Decade, 1987–97

GEOFFREY BEENE

Spring/Summer 1985: Beene's aesthetic (opposite) relied on the physicality of the wearer, using origami-like effects to encapsulate the body.

CHRISTIAN LACROIX

Spring/Summer 1988: Such designers as Christian Lacroix (right) and Thierry Mugler worked to a High Femininity aesthetic in the late 1980s, and celebrated frills and excess with frou-frou dresses and plenty of embellishment.

If fashion in the 1980s was characterized by a sort of schizophrenia, then it was perhaps a sartorial shadowing of the unpredictable shifts in mass consciousness that had been played out across job markets and front pages only a decade before. The revolution in sexual equality and the developments in technology, production, labour and consumption all played their parts in the way people chose to dress.

Once, women's magazines and the style press had hailed the advent of the suit and of a masculinized version of workwear as a method of dressing that would finally allow women to be taken seriously in the workplace. In the late 1980s the press flouted that maxim, finding promise and new direction in the overtly sexualized 'High Femininity' look purveyed by Bob Mackie, Arnold Scaasi, Thierry Mugler and, most prominently, Christian Lacroix (born 1951).

These collections – Lacroix's much-feted debut was in 1987 – were based on puffball skirts, corsetry, babydoll dresses and mini-crinis,

and they were anything but suitable for work. It was seemingly an extreme swing of the pendulum back towards the hyper-female after the masculine aggression that had acted as a subtext to, even a catalyst for, women's clothing for many years, and after many collections of bulky, angular suits. The avant-garde (such designers as Yohji Yamamoto and Rei Kawakubo) had already reacted to 'power dressing', and sought refuge in minimalism by way of formlessness and sombre colours; the mainstream sector of the industry sought to reawaken tastes with florals, frills and a movement that became known as 'frou-frou'.

'Kiss goodbye to those blatant symbols of tough cookie authority', declared US *Cosmopolitan* in 1987. 'The new woman takes centre stage: a new Gigi in a swirl of pastels, her mood is cheeky, precocious and vulnerable.'[1] Commentators have drawn parallels between the movements in fashion during this period and the shifts that took place in womenswear after the Second World War. Having held down jobs while men were at the

Less is ... Pure

DONNA KARAN

1986: Karan endeavoured to assemble the perfect capsule wardrobe for working women by creating elegant essentials for modern life, using stretchy, comfortable and durable fabrics in neutral, toned-down colours.

front lines and far-flung outposts of military authority, women had been reluctant to give up the low-heeled shoes, slacks and unrestrictive undergarments to which they had become accustomed. But what had come next was the New Look, in all its full-skirted, tiny-waisted glory; the 1950s had beckoned – and with them a return to joblessness and drabness, the revival of the Victorian mother myth and the emergence of a compensatory 'feminine mystique' – and hyper-femininity had become hyper-real once more.

Elegant Purism: Donna Karan

If the revolution of gender relations in the 1970s is to be likened to the 'We Can Do It' movement during the war, then Lacroix's High Femininity takes the role of Christian Dior's New Look of 1947. And, as in that original scenario, fashion soon sought an entirely new aesthetic: one that looked completely different and felt completely fresh. From the whittled waists of Dior's circle skirts came the swinging shifts of the 1960s, the unstructured shifts of Pierre Cardin and André Courrèges. Fashion is reactive, so the next possible move from frou-frou had to be something rather more sombre. The latter-day equivalent of the 1960s innovators, and the modern woman's alternative to Lacroix's trussings and Mugler's basques, must then be Donna Karan (born 1948).

Although she is a contemporary of Lacroix, Karan's design directives have always been comfort, ease and practicality. From her early days on the creative team (and eventually as head of design) at Anne Klein, a label known for its sports-derived casual pieces, Karan has always striven 'to design modern clothes for modern people'.[2] She set up her eponymous label in 1985, showing a range of classically cut and tastefully sculpted pieces that were in essence the antithesis to masculine-inspired workwear and power dressing as described by Bob Mackie: 'A lot of women took the tailored

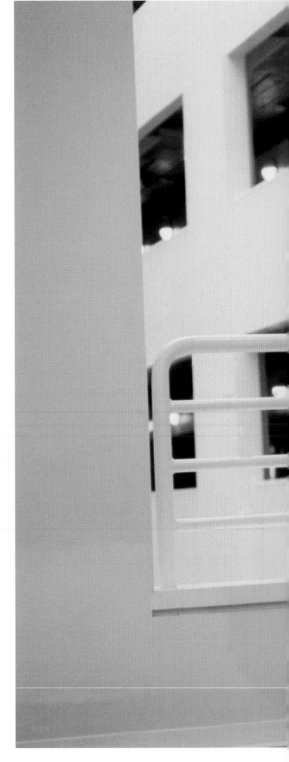

Less is ... Pure

DONNA KARAN

Autumn/Winter 1986–87: Karan's clothes worked to a neoclassical ideal (top left) in order to free up the wearer. Drapery and structureless suiting recall Poiret's and Chanel's work to liberate women through casual clothing.

Resort 1985: In black, with simple fabrics (bottom left), Karan's collections nodded to trends, with wide shoulders and subtle pin-tucking, but were resolutely classic and understated.

Resort 1985: Karan's resurrection of the one-piece bodysuit (right) – originally a garment popularized by the American sportswear designers – was a sign of her determination to integrate separates into a cohesive and practical wardrobe.

look too far, and it became unattractive. Probably, psychologically, it hurt their femininity.'[3]

Cod science apart, Mackie's words are perhaps not far off the mark: that is, women no longer wished to dress as imitation men. This was an undercurrent picked up by *Cosmopolitan*, which asserted that fashion had 'shed its neurotic, aggressive overtone of recent years' and wondered if this signified a 'truce between sexes'.[4] For, whether harmful to the female psyche or not, it was plain to many designers that dressing like a man in order to be treated as his equal was an unsustainable proposition. Women did not necessarily want to look like one of Lacroix's 'happy little virgins who don't want to be virgins', as John Fairchild, the publisher of *Women's Wear Daily*, termed them,[5] but they wanted clothes that felt like a natural uniform rather than a costume or a suit of armour. 'We were wearing pin-stripes', says Karen Bromley, of the Institute of Intimate Apparel. 'We were having this identity crisis and we were dressing like men.'[6]

Donna Karan's restructuring of womenswear was founded on the minimalist idea of reducing the wardrobe to a set of essential garments, first fully explored by the American sportswear designers of the interwar years. The first of many wardrobe 'hits' was her bodysuit, in cotton jersey and a range of neutral colours, designed to be teamed easily with trousers or a skirt, a suit or jeans. Less fussy than a blouse, less starchy than a shirt and less casual than a T-shirt, the bodysuit was smooth and form-flattering without being provocative, and it was functional; there was no danger of it riding up and untucking. Azzedine Alaïa was also marketing bodysuits, as in fact was Mugler, but Karan's was the easiest to slot into an extant wardrobe; it had no trimmings, made no demands on the wearer. It was, she insisted, not part of a fashion-forward statement of aesthetic intent, but designed to make life easier for a swathe of women whose roles had been redefined.

'The bodysuit is basically a T-shirt', Karan later told the press. 'It was about giving women back

their bodies and about giving them back the comfort of their bodies.'[7] It was a minimalist ideal in a time of excess, a mid-point between High Femininity and Masculine Power. And it promised a sartorial Third Way for women the world over, who had been waiting for such a concept – women who were frustrated by mannish tailoring and assiduously not buying into frou-frou.

Karan went on to launch her 'Essentials' line in 1992, a range she termed 'Seven Easy Pieces'. These were interchangeable separates – such as T-shirts, skirts, slacks and blazers – that would all match, and that could be worn in combination to create a fully integrated wardrobe, fitting for any scenario in which the modern woman might find herself. Informed directly by the range created by Claire McCardell for Townley in 1938, Karan's capsule was bought by the daughters of American sportswear, this time not because of any moral directive or austerity measures, but simply because they could and because it would make their lives easier.

Made from such resilient fabrics as jersey and stretch crêpe, Karan's shapes were sophisticated and elegant, softly draped and neatly pin-tucked: a far cry from the arch, structured pieces that had come earlier in the decade. Even the era's signature shoulder pads were reconsidered, reshaped and softened for a silhouette that resembled the curvilinear lines of the female body, without any of the eroticized overtones of the High Femininity movement.

Understated Purism:
Giorgio Armani and Jil Sander

At the same time as Karan was launching her own line, Italian fashion impresario Giorgio Armani (born 1934) was turning his attention to a similar softening technique. Armani, who began as a menswear designer, launched his women's line in 1975 and rode the wave of popularity for androgynous tailoring. The

Less is … Pure

Spring/Summer 1978: By reconfiguring the man's blazer for a woman (right) and dressing models in carefully and simply draped cotton, silk and wool, Armani showed that femininity did not have to mean frothiness.

Spring/Summer 1978: Armani adapted mens' tailoring to the female body (opposite), prompting a move towards greater purism in fashion during the 1980s.

greatest innovation of his early career was the remodelling of a tailored jacket into a gender-neutral garment that would suit both men and women. Streamlining the traditional boxy shape by removing the linings, altering the position of buttons and adjusting the slope of the shoulders, Armani created a minimalist version of tailoring for a new generation of office workers. 'Remember you are women,' he told models backstage at his Spring/Summer 1992 show, 'not young girls walking down the street.' He exhorted them to be 'very elegant, very simple and very natural'.[8]

Indeed, the Armani vision of elegance is one of uncluttered simplicity that takes its inspiration from the Minimalist movement in art, recollecting the lines of a Walter Gropius chair or Donald Judd installation, embracing 'interest' points, but within a strict scheme of rationed extras and balancing acts. Armani pieces are often embellished with fluting, drapery, prints or even beadwork, but never to excess and never to a degree that would render the overall line of the piece or outfit fussy. While there might be colour or adornment, there are no voluminous layers, no puffballs à la Lacroix, no va-va-voom as at Mugler. Armani's work may

Less is ... Pure

Autumn/Winter 1994–95: After the brash power dressing of the 1980s came a softer and quieter take on tailoring for women (opposite, left) – a minimalist version with clean lines, fewer darts and a more mannish fit.

Spring/Summer 1991: Armani's minimalism (opposite, right) stemmed from tailoring, particularly the blazer. This key piece was the basis for any 'pure' ensemble, providing structure and strength.

1997: Actor Jodie Foster was one of many new-generation Hollywood stars who admired the simplicity of Armani's designs, and whose patronage helped propel the Purist look to widespread popularity.

be discreet and sober, but it is not sombre. It is 'an elegance that does not involve "dressing up",' declared *Elle* in 1993, 'and is, above all, easy-to-wear; as he himself put it: "I can't stand any kind of exhibitionism."'[9] Indeed, even staff in his many boutiques must present themselves according to the brand's vision – with strictly no high heels or nail varnish – and the audience are deterred from making too much noise at the biannual shows.

Armani's version of understated luxe tapped into a general feeling that ostentation was on its way out. When high-profile Hollywood names, such as Jodie Foster and Michelle Pfeiffer, began wearing Armani dresses on the red carpet – and to the Oscars, no less – and praising the Italian for his simplicity and sophistication, it became clear that fashion had reached another tipping point. Their garb was not drab or dull, but of the utmost elegance: long-line shift dresses in navy, black or grey silk; spaghetti straps and high necklines; bias cuts and kimono-style detailing. Celebrity had caught up with the tide of fashion, and the sequins, feathers and frills of the late 1980s began to seem like so much flotsam and jetsam.

Spotting the potential for celebrity endorsement, Armani – who was single-minded not only when it came to his design aesthetic and cult of reductivism, but also when it came to business – was the first to have a 'points person' permanently assigned to the West Coast of the United States. It was Wanda McDaniel's job to persuade big names to wear the label's pieces and to make sure the red carpet headcount was high for Armani. With his determined and widespread commercialization of high-end fashion, Armani was truly the designer who first brought minimalism to the masses.

'Purism', as it was dubbed by the style press, became a byword for a discreet, carefully considered elegance, of a sort that did not have the same exclusive and off-puttingly intellectual connotations that such designers as Yamamoto and Kawakubo had accrued. Savvy marketing aside, Armani's and Karan's versions of

Less is ... Pure

minimalism were ultimately so perfect a blend of accessible and aspirational, with their mix of wearability and luxury, that consumers became more aware of them than ever. In the somewhat straitened years of the early 1990s, amid recession and worldwide economic slump, shoppers were focused more than usual on the quality and anonymity of their garments. They wanted something they could wear several times to several occasions over several years. As the excesses of the 1980s receded and were replaced by austerity, ostentatious display became increasingly retrograde; it was tasteless, even thoughtless. Minimalism gained a moral rectitude of a sort it had previously held in wartime (under America's L-85 regulations, for instance, which controlled the use of fabric by stipulating such aspects as skirt length and hem width), and the broader fashion crowd sought a type of purity that was not necessarily puritanical.

German-born Jil Sander (born 1943), who opened her first boutique in 1968 but did not gain true recognition within the international industry until her debut in Paris in 1993, created a range of clothing that displayed more than a little of the archetypal Teutonic tenacity and efficiency. In an apparent volte-face from the gentle femininity towards which Karan and Armani had worked so carefully – and which, indeed, they had had at the forefront of their minds while implementing their aesthetics – Sander went back to androgyny for inspiration for her collections. 'I was looking for a freshness that would be more in tune with modern life', she says. 'My customer was an intelligent woman with self-centred serenity and a radiance of her own. I wanted to free her from fetishistic fashion choices, which subject the body to ornamental narration. There was little decent fashion on the market for a working woman.'[10]

It was a far cry from the power look of the previous decade; Sander's masculine tailoring had none of the Gordon Gekko-style bluster about it. Rather than creating Wall Street dolls in men's suits, she had in her mind an egalitarian simplicity for a new era, a simplicity that was less superficial, and which recognized quality whether or not it was conspicuous in colour or adornment. Her stark tailoring – which, unlike Armani's adapted womenswear mode, changed little from the cut used by bespoke gentlemen's outfitters – included long-sleeved shirts, blazers and tapering trousers that grazed the thighs in the way they were cut, but did not highlight them. Flat shoes were de rigueur.

Sander's line was truly nondescript, but it was made from the very finest wool, silk and threaded cotton. A world emerging from the 1980s was struck by, but ultimately gave in to, paying over the odds for something that looked as though it was nothing at all. Sander calls her design vision 'modern evidence': 'I want to combine the sensual impact of clean lines and elementary forms with the sensibility of the moment', she says. 'Fashion is not about representation and status, but about the best way of invigorating the wearer.' This is clearly a message that many minimalist designers have worked to: from McCardell, Clare Potter and Vera Maxwell, who aimed to create an appropriate persona for a very recently established sector of women, to Kawakubo's empowerment through the use of black, differentiation and negative space. The plainest and most practical types of clothes are the ones that, in their very utilitarianism, broker a previously unimagined existence.

Sander also made it her business to seek out the very newest developments and advances in technofabrics and modern fibres as part of a quest for greater functionality. 'Minimalist fashion turns to … working life, uses durable cloths, applies high-tech solutions, and likes to experiment with one eye on practical purpose', she explains. Her use of neoprene in suits gave them a distinctive shape and robustness, an architectural fluidity that starchy cotton does not have; it also made fabric more durable and long-lasting, ever more impervious to the untold challenges that modern life could throw at the wearer. 'Minimalist design

has a spirit of departure, a sense of economy and a new awareness of the future', she adds.

Sander's work had an ultra-modern feel to it, whereas Karan and Armani could be seen to be continuing a fashion heritage, one of American sportswear and feminine tailoring respectively, of which they were already very much part. Certainly, they revolutionized the industry in their own ways; they are household names in households that perhaps do not otherwise know what is striding along the international catwalks. But Karan based her interpretation of minimalism on the urban-casual sportswear aesthetic that has always dominated the American market and American designers, and Armani looked to the institutionalized Italian, and inherently Catholic, austerity of his ancestors to create a pared-down, everyday elegance.

So what did the Purists share, that they so effectively conquered the fashion scene for almost a decade between 1987 and 1995? What were the rules? 'I would name technical precision', says Sander. 'State-of-the-art materials, comfort, honesty and transparency, harmony, perfectionism in focusing on the best possible solution, and a sharp, contemporary spirit.' These are just as applicable to Armani, Karan and Sander as they are to Chanel, McCardell and Cardin. Concerted movements within fashion are born of a familiar impetus: the desire to keep up. Chanel developed tricot that daywear might be less cumbersome, easier to move in; McCardell reworked the complexities of couture for a mass market; Cardin wanted to be at the forefront of function and, when extant media were not capable of fulfilling his vision, he invented fabric anew.

Of course, the 1990s Purists were not working in a vacuum, any more than Mariano Fortuny was when he looked to neoclassical art for inspiration. Developing their signature looks within the movement, these designers looked for struts to use as a basis for their pieces: Karan to McCardell, and Armani to a heritage of Italian tailoring as well as to Eastern art and tribal influences.

Less is ... Pure

Autumn/Winter 1995–96:
Calvin Klein's collections for
young professionals (right)
became the wardrobe for
an entire demographic,
whispering of an urbane
and austere New York cool.

Spring/Summer 1994: There
was a youthful nonchalance
and glamour to Klein's brand
of minimalism (opposite) that
took the severity of Armani
and the functionalism of
Karan in a different direction
and to new audiences.

Sander's own interest in Madeleine Vionnet,
that high priestess of drapery and unadorned
gracefulness, is evident also. 'My aesthetic goal is
not so minimalist', she admits. 'Form and nature,
silhouette and movement should energize each
other. I think there is a lot of elegance in that.'

Youthful Purism: Calvin Klein

Other designers in the Purist bracket took
inspiration not from fashion's archives, but from
their surroundings. The resurgence of minimalism
during the 1990s was born of a more general
Weltanschauung in terms of consumption, taste
and society, and such designers as Calvin Klein
(born 1942) developed this newly present urban
outlook until it was part of the very fibres of their
collections. Having founded his empire in the
1970s, Klein was originally famous for his jeans,
khakis and all-American vision in a way that the
New York wartime designers had not the means
to be – that is, in a way only mass production on
an immense and international scale could bring.
Klein's inherent American-ness had its basis in
his subversion of streetwear, but it very easily
gave him a utilitarian foundation on which to
build a collection of modern, formal and minimal
clothing suitable for a new generation of young
city-based executives emerging from the
1980s with none of the aesthetic sensibilities
associated with that garish decade.

Klein's first pieces in the Purist vein were
youthful and urban, taking cadence – as Donna
Karan did – from the New York of the early 1990s,
from the panache and class of the younger
workers, who were by now bored with and
contemptuous of the hyperbolic attitudes of the
antecedent Yuppies. A sporty but formal look,
encompassing cocoon coats, dresses, suiting
and casualwear and made from high-resistance
modern fabrics, created a sect of minimalism
that was sleekly and quietly bourgeois, without
being quite as subdued as the versions purveyed

by Armani and Karan. Klein, too, took inspiration from the work of Vionnet, but he also looked to the modern American aesthetic of Halston (1932–1990), whose simplified use of jersey had fused sports-casual with disco-decadence towards the end of the 1970s.

Texture and quality were the most conspicuous angles of Calvin Klein's clothes, which were made from the most hyper-luxurious of fabrics. All other costs he cut to the quick, by removing linings and adornment and carefully constructing pieces from as few swatches of fabric as possible, with single seams, giving intriguing new dimensions to flat-cut clothing. Although his pieces lacked the structural intricacies of Sander's, they were unobtrusive and functional, working in a similar vein to those of McCardell, and engineered intelligently to the machinations of mass production. It was less formal; it was fresh; it was directional and provocative, but in the most tacit way. It looked and felt futuristic but simultaneously chic, paving the way for the likes of Michael Kors and Narciso Rodriguez.

Others were experimenting with the youthful side of Purism, such as Antonio Miro (born 1947), whose plain cotton and jersey ensembles managed to strike a balance between functional and fun, and emitted a restrained sensuality that had so far been absent in the sector. 'I like simple and useful objects, which will accompany me in my daily life and grow old with me,' he once declared, 'like the clothes I design, which are comfortable and austere, and fit so well you could easily forget you were wearing them.'[11] There was Geoffrey Beene (1927–2004), also, who became known for the varied dimension he was able to render in cloth simply through pattern-cutting, and whose collections were based primarily on the system of yin and yang. Making use of reversibility and origami techniques, Beene created slick, figure-hugging single-seam dresses with an attention to the anatomy of the wearer that pointed to a much later version of minimalism. Trained as a doctor, he focused

Less is ... Pure

RIFAT OZBEK

Spring/Summer 1990: Ozbek married clubwear and conscience in an all-white collection of sportswear emblazoned with spiritual phrases. It embodied the lightness and airiness of Purism, as opposed to the sombre tones of the deconstructionists and the avant-garde, and further indicated the extent to which minimalism and morality were linked during the Purist era.

on the body within, and his pieces referenced a similar simplicity of design from a distance, with infinite detail apparent only on closer inspection: *trompe l'œil*, for instance, double-faced fabrics and sophisticated illusions, whereby a dress would suddenly reveal itself to be a skirt and bolero jacket.

Whether the point of a minimalist outlook in fashion is in fact for the wearer to 'forget they are wearing' a garment or to attract attention because of a piece's very nonchalance is much debated. Attention-seeking was certainly not at the heart of the movement as it evolved during the late 1980s and 1990s, but it is clear that designers had a heightened sense of delivering a message, whether social or economic.

Rifat Ozbek (born 1953), a Turkish designer who began showing in London during the 1980s, was among the first to make minimalism political when he eschewed his usual Souk-style aesthetic in favour of an all-white collection, just as Cardin and Courrèges had done in the 1960s, emblazoned with such motifs as 'Nirvana' and 'Serenity'. It was a seminal and striking example of how minimalism could be hard-hitting and conspicuous while adhering to the fundamental principle of a quest for essence, a dichotomy in which that later designers would take much interest. Ozbek was one of the first to publicize, or rather publicly to analyse, minimalism's intrinsic link to mass consumption, globalization and the worldwide economic structure. It was a link that proved essential for the next development of the movement within the industry.

Notes

1 'Bold Shoulders!', *Cosmopolitan* (US), February 1987, p. 22.
2 Ingrid Sischy, *Donna Karan: New York*, London (Thames & Hudson) 1998, p. 16.
3 Quoted in Susan Faludi, *Backlash: The Undeclared War Against American Women*, London (Vintage) 1992, p. 208.
4 'Meet the Feminist Femme Fatale', *Cosmopolitan* (UK), September 1987, pp. 40–41.
5 Quoted in Faludi, *Backlash*, p. 215.
6 Quoted in *ibid.*, p. 208.
7 Quoted in Sischy, *Donna Karan*, p. 15.
8 Quoted in Nicola White, *Giorgio Armani*, London (Carlton) 2000, p. 15.
9 *Ibid.*, p. 17.
10 This and all other quotations from Jil Sander in this chapter are taken from email correspondence between her and the author, May 2010.
11 Quoted in Team Arco, *Minimalism: Minimalist*, Barcelona (Könemann) 2003, p. 147.

Less is ... Less

Minimalism Deconstructed, 1989–99

ANN DEMEULEMEESTER

Autumn/Winter 1988–89: Demeulemeester works in a dark, almost gothic palette, creating dramatic monochrome looks.

With fashion in the 1980s firmly divided between the bourgeois and the avant-garde, two very different types of minimalism began to emerge. The large commercial houses, such as Armani and Donna Karan, opted for chic and clean purism – essential, practical garments that were classically modern, technically complex and luxuriously understated. Smaller labels and younger designers, however, moved minimalism into a more conceptual arena, taking as a precedent not the spare and stark specifications of design, but the inherent physicality of minimizing an object, either at its creation or through its destruction.

Rei Kawakubo and Yohji Yamamoto had already explored the possibilities of a hyperbolic version of minimalism – that is, a paring down to essentials that was proclamatory precisely because of its aggressive negation – and it was this downplayed, lo-fi and often grungy elegance that paved the way for the next stage of minimalism in the late 1980s: deconstruction. It seems paradoxical to discuss minimalism as a means of making an overt statement, but (as with Chanel, André Courrèges and Kawakubo) it is an aesthetic that can have great impact. Given the increasing subculture in the 1980s of 'anti-fashion' – followers of which aimed to opt out of fashion trends and the seasonal circus by choosing sombre, plain and subdued pieces – it was no surprise that a group of designers emerged whose vision was not just innovative and inventive, but also knowingly ironic and humorous. They subverted and mocked the accepted mores of fashion at that time, not satirically, but with all the craftsmanship and artistry of traditional couturiers. 'As a backlash against the established Eighties excesses – and tempered by Mr. Gaultier and the Japanese designers – a new style was born', said Amy Spindler in the *New York Times*. 'It offered a sort of asbestos suit against the bonfire of the vanities.'[1]

Martin Margiela (born 1957) had assisted Jean Paul Gaultier before showing his first catwalk collection in Paris for Spring/Summer 1989. It featured a leather butcher's apron that had been reworked into an elegant cocktail dress, and a tulle ballgown that had been turned into a series of tailored jackets. Models had blackened eyes and pale skin, and they walked down a catwalk of red paint, leaving gory red footprints on a roll of paper that Margiela then used to create the next season's collection. It was a show of anger, some said, 'at what too much money and too little imagination had done to the art form'.[2] Buyers and press were not sure what to make of this fledgling designer from Antwerp, who had poked fun at convention, and in a truly new and imaginative way.

The audience was confounded also by the designer's decision to remain anonymous, steadfastly refusing to give interviews or to take his bow at the end of his shows. Instead, the label was known as Maison Martin Margiela, and the audience could address their admiration only to a team of assistants. Margiela wished to focus attention on the clothes; for the same reason, he often sent models down the catwalk backwards or with gauze-covered faces. But he also emphasized the plurality of vision, acknowledging that his pieces were born of a concerted effort by a team of designers. The point was also to highlight the difference between Margiela and such superstar designers as Giorgio Armani and Ralph Lauren, whose faces were inseparable from their brand identity and ideology.

As fashion became more concerned with labels and branding, the work of Margiela became even more relevant, not only for its technical brilliance and new appraisal of feminine elegance, but also for its values. In the face of the excess of the 1980s, Margiela's anonymity and impersonal approach were anachronistic but well judged, and indicative of his inherently minimalist sensibilities. The label inside a Margiela garment is a blank white rectangle, fixed with four white stitches that are visible on the exterior; his clothes are an anti-fashion, anti-status status symbol – a nudge and a wink between those in the know – and this

Less is ... Less

MAISON MARTIN MARGIELA

Spring/Summer 1990: The use of incongruous and inexpensive fabrics draped to perfection (right) is a signature of the label, creating a low-key version of simple luxury.

Anonymity (right, bottom), both of design and of the designer himself, is key to the Margiela aesthetic.

Spring/Summer 1989: The light, aspirational qualities of the Purists and their work with supermodels and mainstream magazines provided a backdrop for Margiela's breakthrough collection (opposite), in which he covered the models' faces and showed deconstructed tailoring.

quiet sense of inclusiveness sums up the anonymous designer and his paradoxically eponymous label. Although he has now retired, the label continues under the creative direction of his team, and he has perhaps achieved the status of the ultimate fashion minimalist, having given up even his name in the quest for artistic purity.

The Margiela insignia is all in white (or 'whites', in the house's own words) and constructed as a faux dictionary entry, with various 'definitions' of the brand: 'Maison Martin Margiela proper noun, plural, derived from the name of a Belgian stylist. ... Known for its ... transgression ... Categorized successively as underground, deconstructive, destroy, grunge, minimalist ...'.[3] Shops are painted uniformly white inside (and often out) and filled with reclaimed, reinvigorated bits of junk – old sinks, for example, and distressed, salvaged wood – while shop assistants and members of the design team are robed in white coats reminiscent

MAISON MARTIN MARGIELA

Autumn/Winter 2002–03:
A characteristically minimal
handbag as shown (right)
in the label's lookbook,
presented by one of the
house's anonymous design
team dressed in signature
Margiela 'whites'.

Spring/Summer 1993:
Deconstructed tailoring
is another hallmark of the
label, mixing traditional
forms with modern
irreverence. Here (right
bottom), a formal jacket is
held together by gaffer tape.

of those worn by seamstresses and artisanal workers in couture houses at the turn of the twentieth century. By suppressing his own identity, Margiela has created an internationally recognized presence in fashion, carefully and clinically codified.

The house produces eleven lines: the artisanal ranges (couture-style pieces made by hand in Margiela's atelier) are known as '0' and '0+10' for women and men respectively; his ready-to-wear 'collection for women' is '1' and for men is '10' (those are the pieces with blank white labels inside); '4' represents a 'wardrobe for women', designed with comfort in mind; '14' is a 'wardrobe for men' (its intention to put timeless design into practice: the house brings out a replica collection each season); '11' is a range of unisex accessories; '22' is footwear for men and women; 'MM6' is a diffusion ready-to-wear line for women, less avant-garde than '1'; '8' is eyewear; and '13' is a range of various other pieces, including pamphlets and magazines.

Such ordering calls to mind an inventory, but it is also part of a theory not so dissimilar to the attempts of Pierre Cardin and Courrèges to turn a design ethic into an entire lifestyle. Wearing and appreciating clothing by Margiela may not be a mainstream activity, but it could be all-enveloping if one allowed it to be: the ultimate minimalist lifestyle.

Margiela's garments are endlessly complex in construction, although they often appear ripped and shredded beyond repair. There is an argument that minimalism should be manifested in a clean palette, an unfussy garment, a low level of surface detail; much of Margiela's vast *oeuvre* features *trompe l'œil*, holes and unravelling hems. But his design aesthetic – dubbed 'la mode destroy' by commentators at the time – is as reductivist as, say, Jil Sander's contemporaneous vision; as a deconstructivist designer, Margiela was searching for a similar essence, but where Sander created garments from nothing, Margiela's emphasis was on reaching that nothing through a distillation of

MAISON MARTIN MARGIELA

Autumn/Winter 1999–2000:
Margiela explores function
and form with his use
of different media, from
reworking leather aprons
and wigs into garments,
to – below – a duvet coat.

Spring/Summer 2009:
Margiela's twentieth-
anniversary collection
(below, right) revisited
his 'greatest hits', one of
which was the use of *trompe
l'œil* to question the very
physicality of a garment.

Less is … Less

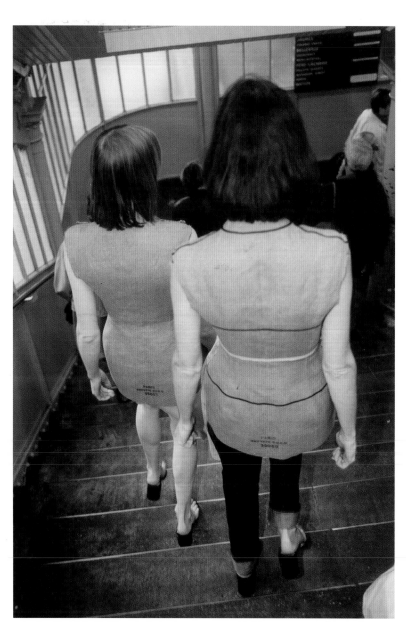

already extant forms. Hence the leather apron of his first collection, and the ballgown; later, painters' canvases became clothing, a disco-ball morphed into an armoured top, wigs were stitched together to make jackets, and, for Autumn/Winter 1999–2000, a 100 per cent down duvet became a coat.

Minimalist fashion for Margiela is about identity and existence – most often about the suppression of one or the other – and these concepts are at the heart of the minimalist dichotomy between form and function. Margiela manipulates both, so that there is a fluidity between them; it is no longer a choice of one over the other. For Autumn/Winter 1989–90, he created a bodice made from the hessian cover of a 1950s tailor's dummy, and showed it on the catwalk over a white cotton blouse, in a bid to highlight the origins, uses and boundaries of clothing. A statement written for Maison Martin Margiela by the designer's business partner, Jenny Meirens, says that the label stands for 'an authenticity: that restores the true or right values of things again'.[4]

Margiela's extended use of *trompe l'œil*, especially in his Spring/Summer 1996 collection, is a further part of his quest for the ultimate codification of fashion: a flesh-toned T-shirt decorated with tattoos recalls the anthropomorphic aspects of Issey Miyake's work, while a cardigan overlaid with a photographic print of a safari jacket raises the sort of existential questions with which minimalism concerns itself. If this cardigan functions to all intents and purposes in the same way as the safari jacket printed on it, which form is the most relevant? Is the cardigan not in fact a cardigan at all, because it has been imbued with the other garment? Margiela's clothes are adept and concise representations of philosophies that are intended to raise questions and negotiate the intractable intricacies associated with minimalism.

Margiela's garments are also reductivist in the traditional sense, in that most feature few

embellishments or surface adornment, are in
sombre colours and display practised plainness.
Decoration and modishness come from cut
and construction: the giant blazers and jackets
of Autumn/Winter 2001–02, for example, or a
Spring/Summer 1991 dress cut from pinstriped
lining fabric, with visible darts and separate
cotton shoulder sections. Margiela also made
pioneering use of the flat cut, not necessarily
to render garments more dynamic or easier to
move in – as Miyake and Yamamoto did – but
to raise aesthetic questions of dimension and
volume. For his Spring/Summer 2009 twentieth-
anniversary collection, a circle of black leather
became a leather jacket, realigning pattern-
cutting methods in the same way that Cardin had
done, but before that Margiela's Spring/Summer
1998 show dealt with flat garments: shirts and

twinsets, with sleeves positioned at the front
rather than the sides to give a crushed effect, and
a sweater that unzips into one large rectangular
piece of cloth. Margiela was as concerned as
Chanel and Miyake with the interaction of body
and space within his garments, but his interest
lay in the extreme ratios of each, rather than
quotidian or pragmatic solutions.

But Margiela's version of minimalism did
in fact deal with the everyday, and that was
where its humour lay: in the abstraction of
existence. His 'Ghosts of Garments' collection for
Spring/Summer 2008 saw shredded jeans and
denim pelmet skirts more hole than whole, with
'vestigial accessories' applied to some pieces:
a handbag stitched into the armpit of a dress,
with the now-redundant strap hanging loosely
down the model's arm, and a purse sewn on to
the front of a skirt. Lapels, buttons and other
detailing were embossed faintly on to collarless
jackets in Margiela's attempt to minimize items
beyond definition.

It was against 'definition' that other
deconstructivists tried to rebel. They shared
Margiela's dissatisfaction with the current mode
of gilt, glamour and women as gilded lilies, and
sought to reinvent notions of elegance, beauty
and taste. Margiela is often conflated with the
Antwerp Six (a group of designers who graduated
from the city's Royal Academy of Fine Arts and
showed their first collections at London Fashion
Week in 1988), but he pre-dates them slightly.
Geert Bruloot, the PR who brought these
designers to the United Kingdom, remembers the
impact they had on the contemporary scene:

*The Japanese were in this deconstruction mood,
and we didn't have that glamour feeling, the light,
colourful style of the Italians. We were very Nordic,
and this gave a dark edge to fashion. When Martin
[Margiela] started coming up with his own line, it
was even worse, because it was presented in very
special places, like car garages and metro stations.
It was literally underground. But also there,
I remember a lot of people from the press didn't*

Less is ... Less

MAISON MARTIN MARGIELA

Autumn/Winter 2006–07: Quiet, pared-down, rough-edged elegance (opposite) is a signature of many Margiela pieces, which owe their structure to drapery and texture.

ANN DEMEULEMEESTER

Autumn/Winter 1988–89: Detailing is often inspired by historic dress and used to reinvigorate traditional tailoring, such as this oversized Edwardian-esque bow collar (right).

understand. They didn't attach to it – 'who's waiting for that?' they said. He moved fashion forward. Twenty years of work and it's as if everything has been done now.[5]

There was shared intention among the group, which included Dries Van Noten and Ann Demeulemeester, to peel away the layers of excess and make clothes that were fundamental and single-minded in their aesthetic.

Utilitarian Gothic: Ann Demeulemeester

Demeulemeester (born 1959) shares Margiela's passion for construction, elegance and intricacy, but her style is more subdued, more classical, and rather more led by tailoring. Margiela's use of raw edging (achieved by recalibrating the sewing machines so the hem overlock is inaccurate) is the main difference between him and Demeulemeester, whose aesthetic – although just as raw and neo-gothic – is more streamlined and tidy. Celebrated for her work in monochrome, Demeulemeester has become known for white shirts, black trousers and long skirts, tailored jackets and cutaway detailing, all worn roughly layered on top of one another and finished with a sturdy pair of bovver boots.

Demeulemeester's clothes often look as if they are falling from the body, but they are secured by internal fastenings and harness, giving her version of elegance a utilitarian edge. She works asymmetrically, uses draping for constructive effect, and experiments with such atypical fabrics as paper, leather and distressed suede. Demeulemeester's take on minimalism is, so to speak, the missing link between the version conceptualized by Margiela, Yamamoto and Kawakubo and that commercialized by Armani, Karan, Calvin Klein and Jil Sander, using functional modern basics and bold colour – especially black – to structure practical but purist ensembles.

'For Ann, black is the most poetic colour', says Kaat Debo, artistic director at Antwerp's Modemuseum and curator of its exhibition *Masters of Black in Fashion and Costume* (which featured more than a few pieces by Demeulemeester). 'It's not a negative colour for her, it has nothing to do with nostalgia or even romanticism. It's just a pure colour.'[6] Black is also an important and permanent colour in Demeulemeester's design process, and she works in little else when cutting and developing the first toiles for garments, testing form and tailoring. If she feels anything is missing beyond that stage, it is then that she might add colour as decoration, or experiment with texture and sheen, but she believes that her designs are often perfect without further embellishment. For Demeulemeester, Debo says, 'black is pure poetry, the most beautiful and mysterious colour.'

The use of black is, of course, an important aspect of minimalism; it is the colour most

ANN DEMEULEMEESTER

Spring/Summer 1996:
Demeulemeester's take on
traditional tailoring brought
minimalism to a grungy new
level (opposite), and cutaway
details, rips, slashes and
origami folds gave it a new
streetwear aesthetic.

Autumn/Winter 1989–90:
Demeulemeester's early
collections (right) were full of
dramatic, imaginative takes
on archetypal menswear –
including cutaway shirts
and the 'drop-from-the-hip'
trousers that were to become
a signature.

frequently associated with the aesthetic, lending a certain ascetic, highbrow edge. Minimalist designers work mainly in neutrals – white, black, stone, nude, grey – because these tones have fewer associations and connotations. The lure of white and black is perhaps indicative of the two minimalist camps in fashion at the outset of the 1990s: the (mainly American and Italian) Purists worked largely, although not exclusively, in white because it emphasized minimalism's sense of lightness, sportiness, comfort and modernity. The deconstructivists preferred black or sombre colours because they were precisely the opposite: serious, less naïve, introspective, unfeminine and somehow purer, with a lack of any sexual connotation. White is, of course, a bridal colour, whereas black, although generally traditionally for mourning, holds no latent meaning that underlies the wearer's sense of femininity. Demeulemeester's use of black in her androgynous tailoring is the ultimate avoidance of gender stereotyping, and caused many fashion journalists to find her work as challenging as Margiela's in the early days of her career.

Demeulemeester's tailoring was sharp but loose-fitting and unstructured, chiming perfectly with the evolving grunge trend of the early 1990s, and her high-necked blouses, bunched sleeves and perennial long and flowing skirts, coats and dresses owed something to the Victorians. Despite her boundary-breaking and modernizing force in fashion at the time, there is often a nostalgia in Demeulemeester's collections, similar in effect to the rural references of Yamamoto and Miyake. Her classic 'drop-from-the-hip' wide-leg trousers make the wearer look fragile and youthful; her skilfully cut soft leather jackets are urban and chic, but retain an armour-like quality in their asymmetrical zip-lines, creating a breastplate effect.

There are nods also to Japanese purity of cut, with tailored white shirts and blouses in wraparound styles, which fasten with an obi-style belt. Demeulemeester's Autumn/Winter

1992–93 collection featured a blouse that referenced both Western and Eastern history of dress, with puffed sleeves atop an obi waist and a daubing of black paint across the front, which looked as much like a distorted Japanese character as an arbitrary spillage. Such manipulation of form as this highlights the fusion of cultures through their most significant garments; in Demeulemeester's hands, the traditional white shirt becomes half-kimono, dhoti trousers are almost skirts, and a monastic-looking jumpsuit has a cutaway back panel, revealing the body in unexpected ways. All quietly done, but all arrestingly modern.

Texture and depth are also key to the minimalism of Demeulemeester, who not only works in cotton and silk, but also sometimes adds embellishment by way of feathers, beads and jewels, all placed with infinite care so as not to overwhelm the outfit. Her Spring/Summer 1992 collection featured feather necklaces paired with baggy pinstriped trousers fastened with cord, and a delicately beaded, cropped silver

ANN DEMEULEMEESTER

Spring/Summer 1993:
Demeulemeester's
pioneering of layered and
deconstructed tailoring
(above) brought a refreshing
modernity and casualness to
the form, making it attractive
to a new generation.

Autumn/Winter 1992–93:
Obi-style belts (above,
right) give new currency to
wardrobe staples, and are
presented with flounced
sleeves and seemingly
accidental spatter prints
to ironize the formality
of a garment.

Autumn/Winter 1990–91:
Demeulemeester applies
her dark, gothic aesthetic
to practical, classic
pieces (opposite).

Less is ... Less

ANN DEMEULEMEESTER

Autumn/Winter 1993–94:
Richly textured fabrics
(right) combine with
Demeulemeester's generally
sparse aesthetic to create a
new version of minimalism,
one driven by muted colours
and a downbeat, almost
grungy, severity.

Autumn/Winter 2003–04:
Demeulemeester's signature
austerity and asceticism are
belied by the complexity of
construction behind much
of her work (below).

waistcoat with a pair of black cotton drawstring trousers. Both were statement looks, but they retained a quiet minimalist elegance. Such adornment is seemingly impossible to place in a way that ensures a garment remains minimalist in aesthetic, but Demeulemeester's additions repeatedly make garments appear even more austere. Despite her penchant for black and feather trim, there is little gothic about her work; her pieces are too clean, too unfussy, too full of righteous attitude. She is a minimalist through and through, and one who has influenced the current revival of the aesthetic more than most.

Demeulemeester's aesthetic owes much not only to her infinite skill as a pattern-cutter and artist, but also to her visionary sense of styled separates. Rather than dictating a head-to-toe 'look' in the way that Christian Dior had, and as Armani and Sander were still doing at the time, Demeulemeester quite reasonably worked on the assumption that her clothes could be worn with other pieces. She worked backwards from the notion of an all-encompassing minimalist lifestyle provided by only one designer, and took minimalism in a more realistic, less extreme and ultimately more credible direction. Karan and, before her, Claire McCardell had, of course, designed ranges of separates, but theirs were created specifically to be worn together. Demeulemeester's was the first true incarnation of minimalist streetwear – of essentials rather than ensembles, of tailored separates rather than a total outfit – styled, as always, to seem as casual and noncommittal as possible, with none of the extremities of the designed-to-shock Comme des Garçons or Margiela shows.

Avant-garde Timelessness: Helmut Lang

This mix of high and low, of tailoring with sportier pieces and separates, was to become fundamental to minimalism, and it was Helmut Lang (born 1956) who made it intrinsic to his aesthetic of sleek, attenuated citywear. His mixture of luxury fabrics with newly developed synthetics and commonly derided cheaper materials created a schizoid layered look that, although not deconstructed in the most obvious sense, went some way to breaking the hegemony of tailored separates. It seems odd now to think of a time when a vest worn with stretch-fabric trousers was revolutionary, but Lang is in the same category as Karan and McCardell when it comes to chic, comfortable clothing designed to be fundamental to the modern wardrobe.

Lang's entrance into fashion came in 1977 when, after fruitlessly attempting to buy the perfect white T-shirt, he created his own. This anecdote sums up his collections of 'deceptively simple pieces that have always seemed so authentically "of the street" and yet utterly classic', as Vogue described them in 1998.[7] 'Lang's designs always appeared, at first glance, incredibly conservative', says fashion writer Iain R. Webb. 'They were modest and not at all showy – this provided an alternative way to dress, coming as it did on the crest of the high-gloss, hi-octane glamour embodied by Lacroix, Versace and the Supermodels.'[8]

Lang created a look that became almost ubiquitous. It was a version of post-grunge chic; he understood the dissatisfaction with the bourgeois precepts challenged by the likes of Margiela and Kawakubo, but he reflected it in a less provocative and more socialized way. By the early 1990s, consumers were looking for a new fashion formula, and Lang was the designer who offered it to them, showing his first collection in Paris in 1986, before making a name for himself in the United States some years later. 'He's the world's most subtle rebel', said photographer Elfie Semotan.[9]

Distinctly avant-garde, Lang paid little heed to established methods, backing silk with nylon to create fluid, shimmering textures, and making garments from unexpected media, such as PVC

Less is ... Less

HELMUT LANG

Autumn/Winter 1999–2000: Lang's all-encompassing vision of womenswear, down to arm gauntlets, belts and cummerbunds (right), was akin to that of the space-age designers of the 1960s, who envisioned an entire utilitarian lifestyle to go with their clothes.

Autumn/Winter 1990–91: Lang's aesthetic was deliberately lo-fi (opposite, top left). His intention was to create a comfortable but strikingly modern uniform.

Autumn/Winter 1993–94: Stretch cotton and jersey made for collections that were wearable and nonchalant (opposite, top right), with highly constructive bondage detailing that spoke of a distinctly urban aesthetic.

Autumn/Winter 1995–96: Minimal tailoring in the classic vein was styled alongside futuristic details (opposite, bottom left) inspired by urban life and 1990s clubwear.

Autumn/Winter 1997–98: Unexpected fabric choices (opposite, bottom right) – shiny and industrial, or worn and distressed – gave Lang's collection a modern edge.

for trousers and net for vests and T-shirts. Everything was sharply cut to ensure androgyny, and cocktail and column dresses were made from jersey and cotton in a subversion of formality. 'The mood was reinforced by Lang's use of expensive fabrication', continues Webb. 'Cashmere, wool and silk. However by mixing these fabrics with nylon, ciré, neoprene and rubber, he kept it modern.'

Lang's clothes were challenging in their inversion of fashion codes. He created impact with streamlined, sinuous and sensual lines rather than with embellishment, and he did not seek to create femininity in his collections. Rather, he liberated a generation of women from the fetters of looking 'striking' or making an aesthetic statement, by producing precisely the opposite reaction. His cuts were timeless but his pieces immediate: a pair of cigarette-cut trousers from a collection of 1992, made from a synthetic stretch material in bright scarlet, were shown with a halterneck top and breastplate, throwing the delineation between day- and eveningwear into turmoil.

The pieces were not occasionwear; they were clothes for an army of urban warriors to wear throughout their waking hours. They marked something of a return to the 'lifestyle minimalism' invented in the 1960s and perpetuated by the Japanese: Helmut Lang was a way of life as well as a system of dressing. In fact, he produced one of the first coherent systems of ensembles, created with reference to the tiniest of details. Catwalk looks were embellished with harnesses and body straps, separate waistbands and wrist ties, all layered carefully to create his singular aesthetic. 'His clothes, and the way he presented them – on a minimal runway, with men and women, some of whom were friends from Vienna – had an opaqueness and sexual tension that was new and, unlike grunge, very grown up', recalls Cathy Horyn.[10]

Lang also made use in womenswear of fabrics and cuts associated with menswear, as Chanel and Sander had pioneered, adapting a narrower

suit line that took fashion away from its power-dressing shoulders-and-lapels dogma. He eschewed the opulent and the inflammatory, asking make-up artists at his shows to create models who looked simply and naturally dewy, fresh and beautiful. Lang was a woman's designer in the same way as Karan, and liked the idea of making women's lives simpler without taking away the fun and sartorial flair that fashion could provide.

'There's total evolution, conviction and honesty in the way he designs', said photographer Juergen Teller in 1998. 'From season to season the clothes never jump arbitrarily from one thing to another. You never get the sense with Helmut, the way you do with some other designers, that he feels he has to change for the sake of it.'[11] Indeed, Lang worked according to a concept that he called 'a non-referential view of fashion', meaning that he was not influenced by past or received dictates of dress, and that he created basic garments that were right for the zeitgeist.[12] This, of course, also meant that he did not design according to trends or fads; instead, his collections were always dominated by his signature attenuated lines, layering and versatility, and although colours and structure might change between seasons, little else did. It is a distinction among minimalist fashion designers that they are rarely influenced by trends and have a signature aesthetic that remains key until they feel they have worked through it in a thorough and exhaustive way.

Minimalism Enters the Mainstream: Miuccia Prada

The 1990s continued in the anti-fashion and anti-status vein, and it was this outlook that created the climate in which that of Miuccia Prada (born 1949) became one of the most sought-after but understated names in fashion. Her range of totes and rucksacks, made from a military-specification nylon that was tough and doubly reinforced, was the final word in status

symbol, and yet subtle and anti-status. It was the popularization of Prada that finally brought minimalism into the mainstream arena, and Miuccia Prada's vision of a slick and practical, pared-down city sportswear became the utilitarian version of minimalism that was recognizable and familiar for so long. It was, in fact, until very recently the key interpretation, to a non-industry audience, of minimalism in fashion.

'Careful observation of and curiosity about the world, society, and culture are at the core of Prada's creativity and modernity', reads Prada's mission statement. 'This pursuit has ... introduced a new way to create a natural, almost fashionless fashion.'[13] Certainly, Miuccia Prada's background in political thought (she studied politics and was a fully paid-up member of the Communist Party) has informed her take on modern femininity, which traverses the aesthetic scale from lipstick-print dirndl skirts via silk hotpants and fairy-print cheongsams to linen-mix crop tops woven with gold thread. But the label's earlier collections presented a slick and urbane androgyny that tallied with that of Lang, except in its lack of sex appeal.

Prada's clothes are often naïve and youthful, seemingly based on the wardrobe of a young girl, with knee-high socks, knee-length skirts (a signature length that the brand introduced on to the fashion scene in the mid-1990s) and demure-looking schoolgirl coats in brushed wool. But from Autumn/Winter 1994–95 until Spring/Summer 1999, the label focused this youthful naïvety on providing the ultimate urban uniform. Pieces were childish in construction, flat-cut and simple in colour, ranging mostly from white to beige and cream to grey. They were known as 'uniforms for the slightly disenfranchised', and they made no claims about femininity or vulnerability, nor did they project status openly.[14] 'Prada's minimalism is followed like a Zen Buddhist religion by fashion acolytes', said Suzy Menkes. 'The Prada philosophy fits the (fairly expensive) bill for the Nineties shopper who aspires to be a

PRADA

Spring/Summer 1998:
Developing the unisex
tailoring of the Purists (right),
Miuccia Prada created an
understated modern vision
of smart utilitarianism, a
return to the practicality
so strongly associated
with the movement.

Autumn/Winter 1998–99:
Prada's designs of the 1990s
(far right) recalled the Purism
of earlier in the decade,
but added a grown-up
girlishness to the aesthetic,
which was cleverly undercut
by sparse shapes and a
certain rigidity to guard
against connotations of
vulnerability.

Spring/Summer 1999:
Functionalism informed
the new utilitarianism
(right, bottom) and
brought the potential for
embellishment – but only
what was strictly necessary,
of course.

connoisseur of good things rather than an avid consumer of status symbols.'[15] The garments also shared a can-do attitude with Chanel's early pieces: they were about simplifying existence and reducing complexities.

Prada's clothes did this with reference to actual feminine existence, just as the capsules of Karan and McCardell had done. But they also provided solutions: skirts came with attached hip belts and lightweight detachable pockets that could be worn as money belts and bumbags; coats and jackets were riddled with pockets in unexpected places. Shapes were simple and nostalgic, stark without being severe because of the peppering of girlish references – princess coats, belted jackets, deep-set sailor collars. These collections were as nostalgic as Lang's were non-referential, but they drove the general aesthetic forward rather than sparking a retrograde movement.

In terms of opening up minimalism beyond the catwalk, these Prada collections of 1994–99 were crucial. Not long afterwards, the high street picked up on this modish form of utility clothing and began to copy the drawstring jersey skirts, nylon windcheaters and silk-nylon shifts. The materials were nowhere near as luxurious as those of the Prada versions, but they swiftly changed the way the bulk of shoppers thought about clothing, and minimalism made a return to the mainstream, just as it had at the very peak of the American sportswear era. The emphasis was once more on pragmatic modern clothing options rather than superficially impressive showpieces, and the influence of Prada on the movement was to make it not only universal at the time, but also focused more on practicality than on aesthetic reduction.

PRADA

Autumn/Winter 1999–2000:
Prada's utilitarian aesthetic
gave a new and urban
sleekness (opposite),
combining the practicality of
sportswear with the elegance
and highly visual style of
modern designer fashion.

Spring/Summer 1995: After
the distinctly rough-hewn,
urban trends, Prada's more
feminine interpretation of
minimalism (below) gave new
direction to the aesthetic.

Notes
1 Amy M. Spindler, 'Coming Apart', *New York Times*,
   25 July 1993.
2 *Ibid*.
3 *Maison Martin Margiela: 20: The Exhibition*, exh. cat. by Bob
   Verhelst and Kaat Debo, Antwerp (Modemuseum) 2008.
4 Quoted in *Contemporary Fashion*, ed. Taryn Benbow-
   Pfalzgraf, Detroit (St James Press) 2002, p. 448.
5 Conversation with Geert Bruloot, September 2010.
6 Conversation with Kaat Debo, May 2010. The exhibition
   ran from 25 March to 8 August 2010.
7 Lisa Armstrong, 'The Austrian Empire', *Vogue* (UK),
   September 1998, p. 318.
8 This and all other quotations from Iain R. Webb in this
   chapter are taken from email correspondence between
   him and the author, June 2010.
9 Quoted in Armstrong, 'The Austrian Empire', p. 318.
10 Cathy Horyn, 'Melanie', *The Gentlewoman* 0
   (Autumn/Winter 2009–10), p. 124.
11 Quoted in Armstrong, 'The Austrian Empire', p. 321.
12 Quoted in Benbow-Pfalzgraf, *Contemporary Fashion*,
   p. 404.
13 Miuccia Prada and Patrizio Bertelli, *Prada*, New York
   (Abrams) 2009, p. 9.
14 Mimi Spencer, 'Prada People Power', *Vogue* (UK),
   March 1995, p. 24.
15 Quoted in *ibid.*, p. 25.

Less is ... Glamour

The Return of 'Pretty', 1998–2008

ROLAND MOURET

Autumn/Winter 2005–06: Mouret's Galaxy dress became an iconic part of modern minimalism for its instant but low-key glamour and sex appeal, and for its elaborate system of helpful underpinnings.

After the popularity of the city-inspired minimalism of Miuccia Prada and Helmut Lang came a renewed interest in sportswear, and particularly in redefining it within more formalized fashion codes. In the wake of the 'Hiroshima chic' of the 1980s and the 'heroin chic' of the early 1990s, there arrived a triumphant new aesthetic more obviously in keeping with the recently charted economic upturn, and rather more reflective of the optimistic spirit that had been lacking for several years.

The Japanese minimalists and the deconstructivists had been concerned with a paucity of imagination associated with the commercial and cultural excesses of the 1980s. Recession had brought a harder, more severe and more considered feel to womenswear, either serious or puritanical – neither of which fitted in easily with traditional notions of beauty, sexiness or allure. But as the grip of the original Purists on mainstream fashion began to wane, and as the nonchalance and haphazard slickness of the deconstructivists began to exert a subtle influence from the sidelines, minimalism underwent yet another transformation, and proved its relevance once more.

The resultant marriage of the two divergent strands – which had previously existed very separately – was dubbed 'pretty minimalism' by *Vogue* in 1998; it was a version that skimped on embellishment and decoration without compromising its sense of simple femininity. 'Ann Demeulemeester's lovely hymn to black and white makes a strong case for the new, pretty minimalism', *Vogue* continued. 'Like Sander, Demeulemeester and Comme des Garçons, Helmut Lang shows how minimalism can move forward in a decorative, romantic way: gauzy wool layers, ruffled nylon dresses, gladiator-pleat skirts and baby blue.'[1] It is a measure of the reaction to the new social climate that even the architects of austerity were softening their looks at this juncture.

Although we have seen that most incarnations of the reductivist aesthetic have had some link or other to the status of women's empowerment or the exigencies of modern feminine existence, the style had, prior to this point, been more concerned with playing down the importance of the body, if not disguising it entirely. Not since the days of Christian Dior had there been such an interest in the physicality of clothing and the female body, and, where the New Look of 1947 had contorted, padded and generally manipulated the wearer into a given form, the pretty minimalism of the 1990s – which took sportswear as its base – celebrated a natural and easy style of beauty and elegance, one that relied on an active, urban lifestyle in much the same way as the traditional American sportswear of the 1930s and 1940s had.

The new minimalism was also similarly reliant on money being part of the aesthetic, given its distinctive WASP identity and rather tightly focused Upper East Side demographic. It continued the modern, urban and practical – specifically New York – feel of Donna Karan's and Lang's lines, and matched it with the elegance and feminine refinement of Dior and Cristóbal Balenciaga, even of the early work of Pierre Cardin. But it also injected the aesthetic with a new sexiness – the sensuous simplicity of Halston – and a sense of body-consciousness that had been alluded to by the avant-gardists, but which had not been commercially right until this moment.

Where Yohji Yamamoto and Rei Kawakubo had swathed their models in their infamous 'Jap wraps' – multiple layers of wound cloths transfigured with anonymous lumps, bumps and humps to obscure traditionally feminine visual reference points (such as the hips, waist and breasts) – the pretty minimalists' intentions were to emphasize little else: within a scheme of subdued and sophisticated sexuality, of course. Superficially there may be little to ally Issey Miyake's work with that of Michael Kors and Narciso Rodriguez, but all three are designers who combine a pared-down simplicity of silhouette and palette with a close attention to physicality and the way garments move on the body.

The difference is, of course, with what or whose body the designer is concerned: the cult of extreme thinness at the outset of the 1990s and the grunge-inspired vogue for pallid, fragile-looking models had receded, and an interest in a more athletic – specifically, a more gym-honed – physique had replaced it. The fashion body at that time was bourgeois once again, and whispered of personal trainers in its litheness, exotic holidays with its rich, deep tan, and good breeding in its statuesque (mainly Caucasian) elegance. It was also youthful (although not so youthful as to be swayed by pop movements or the shock of the new) and urbane, inhabiting with confidence a bustling metropolis. The body was liberated from the swathing and swagging, as well as the sharp cuts and power looks, of the 1980s just as society had been liberated from the oppressive recession it had been suffering, and the concomitant austere aesthetic. Pretty minimalism negated the overriding sense of self-righteousness and intellectual superiority for which the movement had gained a reputation during its time as an avant-garde subculture. It was rehabilitated and socialized, with a pop of colour and a flash of leg.

Bold Luxury: Michael Kors

Kors (born 1959) had established his own label in the early 1980s, and was very popular, but he suffered in the recession at the end of the decade, and it was not until his label was refinanced and reorganized in 1993, and he took over as creative director of the prestigious French house Céline, that his profile became what it is today. Latterly he has even featured on such TV shows as 'Project Runway', and it is fair to say that he has smashed the popular image of the minimalist designer as an abstruse and Arctic totem who speaks to no one, issuing opaque metaphorical statements and expecting a cult-like following. 'Mr Kors has shown that simple doesn't have to be zero', said the New York Times in 1988.[2]

Kors claims his designs are born of his hybrid personality: on the one hand, his Swedish Lutheran mother, who inspires his taste for simple, classic pieces, and on the other, his Jewish grandmother, whose taste for the flamboyant is behind Kors's bold colours and distinctly luxe philosophy. 'When I create my collections, I always think about glamour and how to apply it to real life', he says. 'I don't consider myself a minimalist – more of a pragmatist, in that my clothes are based on simplicity of line but always with the inherent versatility of American sportswear.'[3] He was the designer who dared to suggest that women abandon tights in winter, showing short shift dresses on models with defiantly suntanned legs; his customers, of course, are not the sort to be found shivering at a bus stop in the rain. 'Something should be unexpected,' he says, 'but at the same time, timeless. Most clothes should be seasonless – things have to be versatile.'

This versatility is at the heart of Kors's brand of minimalism. His commercial success lies in the fact that his pieces can work for almost any customer. 'For someone with a more classic point of view, my clothes represent something sleek and sophisticated but still within her realm', he explains. 'The same pieces work for a more avant-garde client as her wardrobe staples.' Kors's clothes always manage to remain functional: there is no artifice to them, no instructions needed or complex fastenings. Everything is easily elegant, gracefully simple and artistically pure, addressing the needs and dimensions of the body with stretchy, soft fabrics that envelop and cling, emphasizing the importance in his work of human proportion. His aim is to make women feel as comfortable in a formal dress as they would in a tracksuit, as evinced by First Lady Michelle Obama's decision to wear Michael Kors for her first official portrait, in 2009. 'Talk about modern: she wore a black racer-cut matte jersey dress. Some people say she was channelling Jackie O', he said in an

MICHAEL KORS

(Clockwise from top left)
Spring/Summer 2001;
Autumn/Winter 2000–01;
Spring/Summer 2003;
Autumn/Winter 2006–07:
Kors's brand of sleek
minimalism mixes uptown
luxury with traditional
American preppiness
to produce an elegant,
feminine and modern take
on timeless classics.

interview. 'But Jackie O was never in matte jersey with an athletic cut.'[4]

It is this combination of comfort and chic that sums up Kors's design profile, following once more from his preoccupation with the body in motion. While traditional, architectural minimalism aims to divest itself of the personal, Kors's version accepts that the body is an integral part of the design itself. Michelle Obama's choice of dress for her portrait is indicative of the modern lifestyle into which Kors has tapped. He aims to make life easier for women, while simultaneously trying to smarten everyone up a little. Kors claims that Jackie O is his perfect woman, the woman for whom he makes clothes: her own pared-down sense of style was ostentatious in its powerful combination of glamour and sobriety, and she was among the first to dress in this way. His enthusiastic and sensual interpretations of her look were a hit with shoppers who were just letting go of their beliefs that purism had to come in neutral tones and spare, boxy cuts.

Kors is not averse to using patterns in his collections, but he works most often with full bleeds of colour. Lime-green, fuchsia and bright yellow are signature shades, and are luxurious in their intensity on cashmere, leather and fine wool for autumn and winter, and on cotton and silk for spring and summer. 'Clean lines and unadorned shapes need to be cut in beautiful fabrics, be beautifully finished and perfectly tailored to separate them from the purely utilitarian', he explains. Layering is also key, taking the inventive and nonchalantly elegant styling of separates from the tradition newly created by Demeulemeester and Lang, mixing media and fabrics to create a textured and complex look, striking in its streamlined nature and tonal variety – but with an overriding sense of harmony and simplicity.

In common with Karan and Claire McCardell before her, Kors has made use of the bodysuit in his collections, establishing himself well within the ideology and tradition of the classic American

sportswear designer. And, as did Karan and McCardell, he has pioneered the use of modern fabrics designed to allow optimum mobility and versatility. Kors is vocal in his admiration for McCardell's clothes: 'They were timeless. She was the first designer to look not to Paris for inspiration but to the needs of the American woman.'[5] He also incorporates the traditional American aesthetic into his collections, showing a vast variety of trousers, twinsets and tailored blouses.

But as well as nostalgia for the golden age of American fashion, Kors romantically references the drawing-room ease and glamour of the 1930s more generally. His sportswear-inspired pieces are flattering on the body precisely because of the narrow silhouette they create around it, dropping from shoulder and waist in clean, unaffected lines; dresses are made of such retro fabrics as shantung silk to achieve the old-fashioned effect, although it is made irrevocably modern by Kors's colour choices. His pieces also look to the established femininity of the 1950s in their preppiness, but a restraint inherent in the design keeps them from being vintage-looking or wistfully historicist.

The sexuality of Kors's clothes is an integral part of their complexity and commercial appeal. They never feel ostentatiously alluring, because of their simple cuts and restrained lines, but the clinging silk cowl-necked cocktail dress from his Autumn/Winter 2000–01 collection, for example, is hardly naïve. Similarly, his trademark bare-shouldered shifts and backless slips are fully responsive to their wearer's curves, but a cunning cover-up by way of a jacket, cardigan or bolero renders them acceptable officewear. According to Kors, 'great fashion that works in real life is very similar to the balance in a great meal – too much richness can be overwhelming and totally monastic can seem bland and boring. Balance is everything.' Kors is an American designer with the American woman – and her mischievous side – in mind. But he also follows Lang's trail of non-referential fashion, which is something to which

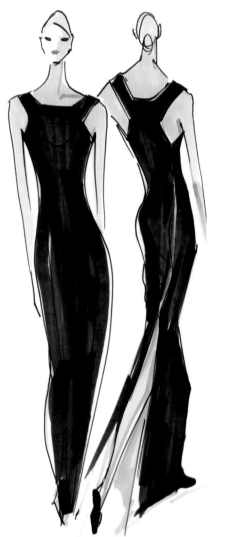
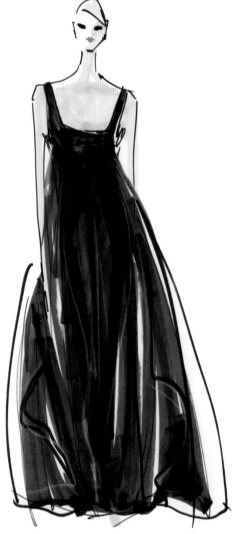

Spring/Summer 2006: Rodriguez's designs (right and overleaf) encapsulate a soft and feminine romanticism with the pragmatics of a modern, urban lifestyle. Clean lines and delicate fabrics, such as chiffon and silk, conspire to create individual but gently minimalist glamour.

minimalist design must adhere if it is to remain relevant in an age of trends that are quick to change, and seasons now blurred by transitory 'resort', 'cruise' and 'pre-' collections.

Pretty Purism: Narciso Rodriguez

Timelessness is a theme echoed by Rodriguez (born 1961), whose own brand of reductivist but glamorous womenswear tallies with the trend of pretty minimalism, although he prefers to retain the earlier term of 'purism' with reference to his own work. 'Minimalism to me always sounds like the work is barren and has a lack of detail', he says. 'Purism is about paring down to the essential – it takes a great deal of thinking to create something pure.'[6] It is precisely this thinking, along with a sense of practicality and logic, that has become a signature in Rodriguez's collections. A blend of a gentle and romantic type

of femininity with a pragmatic urban look is not easily achieved, but it has been part of the designer's repertoire since he took over as creative director at the Italian house Cerruti in 1995.

'Rodriguez has transported an essentially American fashion sensibility (clean, pared-down, desirable) to an established European house and instantly catapulted it into the limelight', said *Vogue* after his first collection for Cerruti.[7] He was part of a nascent movement that looked at models as if they were real women, not in their rail-thin physique and ethereal good looks, but in their off-duty nonchalance between shows and castings. He, along with Marc Jacobs and many others, made this the DNA of his brand: separates that were easily accommodated into already packed wardrobes, and pared-back cocktail dresses for any occasion, pieces that would work timelessly because of their plainness and versatility. Stark and 'barren' are not exactly Rodriguez's watchwords, but he works from a blank canvas of luxury.

The pretty minimalists' main strength was, and is, their commercial viability, of course. Their pieces are universally highly considered by shoppers, buyers and press alike: chic, classic, sophisticated, aspirational, they have little about them that could be devalued at any point in the future. The very worst one could accuse them of being is boring, but even that seems unlikely, given the construction and consideration that goes into making them. Rodriguez trained first under Karan as women's design director at Anne Klein, before moving to the womenswear department of Calvin Klein. In 1996 (the year before he launched his own label) he designed the wedding dress of his friend Carolyn Bessette Kennedy, for her marriage to John F. Kennedy, Jr, and it was then that the wider audience of style pundits took note of his name. The dress in question was of sinuous white silk, bias-cut to the narrow and fluid line that would later become Rodriguez's signature and with no surface decoration to speak of. It clung to the body in motion without revealing flesh or impeding movement.

Rodriguez has described his aesthetic as 'Latin' because of its attention to womanly curves, and as 'urban couture' because of the perennial importance to his work of the citified female identity. While Kors is a body-conscious designer, celebrating the body beneath in his hemlines, sleevelessness and use of colour, Rodriguez is a body-compulsive one: his patterns are deliberately cut to skim the bust and hips in a sensuous and clingy – but not too clingy – way. 'My inspiration comes from keeping my eyes open', he says. 'On the street in urban environments, on the beach where the body is bared and in motion, watching how people move, how they choose to present themselves.' That presentation, in his eyes, shares the luxury and understated sophistication of Kors, but eschews the bold and bright tones that Kors uses, preferring instead nudes; where colour does appear, it comes in rather more romantic and subtle shades. Rodriguez's first own-label collection, for Spring/Summer 1998,

NARCISO RODRIGUEZ

Autumn/Winter 2000–01
(above); Autumn/Winter
2001–02 (right): Separates
are also treated minimally,
and even traditionally
structural forms are pared
back; collarless pieces and
integrated lapels are common
in Rodriguez's collections.

Actor Claire Danes wears
a Rodriguez gown at the
2007 Pratt Fashion Icon
award ceremony.

was awarded the prize for 'cleverest coup' in
Vogue, for 'all those who made pink look edgy,
with top marks going to Narciso Rodriguez'.[8]

Indeed, Rodriguez may design for women, but
his clothes are known for their girlish references
– those pinks in question, of course, from his first
collection, and his fluid silk dresses, floor-length
and flowing. He renders his femininity in tailoring,
too, frequently softened by a lack of structure:
the collarless and lapel-less black cocoon jacket,
unmistakably Japanese in origin, from his
Autumn/Winter 2000–01 collection, or the black
wool greatcoat, caught on the hips with a plain
leather belt, that opened his Autumn/Winter
2001–02 show. The silhouette of the former
look pervaded the collection that followed, from
gilets to blousons to shift dresses. Rodriguez's
signature look is also ultimately less styled
than that of Kors, who presents his layered
ensembles teamed right down to the handbag
and sunglasses; models in a Narciso show rarely
carry any fashion ephemera with them, but are
stripped back to their essential outfits.

Rodriguez has also tapped into a rise in
occasionwear. Just as Giorgio Armani had
foreseen the importance of red-carpet dressing
and created pieces in each collection with that in
mind, Rodriguez's garments have proven perfect
for a new generation of stars who want simple,
fuss-free glamour for the red carpet in colours
that are fun, bright, feminine and not too serious.
'I strive to create beautiful fashion that is both
practical and realistic,' he says, 'so that each
season there are the most desirable pieces in the
collection for women to own and wear for years to
come.' He has dressed the likes of Kate Winslet,
Claire Danes, Eva Longoria and Jessica Alba, and
has become a household name in America, just
as Kors has. Rodriguez's label is a byword for
a type of glamour that is sophisticated without
being snooty, pretty without being frothy and
accessible without being too inconspicuous.

Indeed, the amount of construction that goes
into a Rodriguez gown is all but invisible to the

NARCISO RODRIGUEZ

Spring/Summer 2006: The uncomplicated elegance of Rodriguez's signature full-length pieces was emblematic of a change in fashionable sensibilities, once more towards a quieter sense of glamour and luxury.

untrained eye: his pieces are sculptural in their simplicity. They have to be, in order to create those sinuous and body-hugging lines for which he has become known. 'I love architecture, design, detail, cut, fit, silhouette and beauty', he admits. 'These are characteristics of my work that are a constant and constantly evolving.' The spaghetti straps of his early collections were designed to hold aloft metres of rich, shining silk; his body-conscious jersey dresses fit just so, and yet incorporate panels of colour and tensile strength to ensure the fit does not stretch or go awry, but is subtly perfect at all times. It is unsurprising, and indicative of the success of Rodriguez's design philosophy, that Michelle Obama chose to wear his black-and-red printed shift dress on election night in 2008. It is representative also of his being a thoroughly American designer; the direction 'pretty minimalism' took after the purism of the 1990s was almost entirely American in ideology, with its notions of comfort matched with sassiness.

European Glamour: Roland Mouret

It is interesting to note, then, that the next incarnation of glamorous minimalism was inherently Parisian in its smoky-eyed sex appeal, risqué sheers and Grecian drapery. But clothes by Roland Mouret (born 1962) were, in the first instance, also a natural home for the chic, modern socialite, and, despite their overtly classical aesthetic, there was an athleticism present in his collections that European minimalism had not yet embraced. Everything about them was distinctly high-fashion, with long skirts, sheer blouses and rarefied colour choices that included cerulean and chartreuse, and yet they were also winningly modern, cut to allow the wearer her freedom and to make an impression. Mouret's collection for Autumn/Winter 2000–01, shown in London, featured an asymmetrical dress cut low to expose one breast and a sequinned pastie worn over the exposed nipple. Any previous sobriety

ROLAND MOURET

Spring/Summer 2009:
Cocktail-hour glamour
is given the reductivist
treatment at the hands
of Mouret, whose origami
folding and pin-tucking
give body-conscious form
to dresses and separates.

Less is ... Glamour

ROLAND MOURET

Autumn/Winter 2000–01: Mouret's collections are defiantly sensual and feminized, but his clothes are simple, usually with only one colour per garment and most often unadorned.

associated with minimalism had been shaken off with its reincarnation at Mouret's hands; his collections were defiantly sensual and hyper-feminine, emphasizing waists and breasts in a classical, archetypal fashion. But although the idea of his pieces being 'toned down' in style may seem paradoxical, Mouret's technique and finished garments are still fully deserving of the reductivist tag.

Describing himself as a 'draper', rather than a 'designer', Mouret works – as do Yamamoto and Kawakubo – first and foremost according to the exigencies of his fabric. His signature structured drapery derives from the easy chic of Halston and the sensual, intuitive pattern-cutting of Yves Saint Laurent. 'I love to combine glamour, which is about a trick of the eye and seduction, with a practical type of uniform', he explains. 'That's what I feel my aesthetic is all about.'[9] This combination is essentially anathema to the traditions of American sportswear, which is what makes Mouret's take distinctly European. It brings a sensuality to minimalism, and a sexuality (that is, a gender) that is not allied with athleticism, functionality or motion. Previous reductivist takes by Claire McCardell, Mildred Orrick and even Pierre Cardin had been infused less with the physicality of the female body than with its physical capabilities, and at the height of 'Hiroshima chic', designers ironized the female form in order to remove it safely from the male hegemony. The work of previous body-conscious designers, such as Azzedine Alaïa, who worked in black, brown and other sober colours, had nevertheless been tempered by an overt sexuality that meant it could not be technically classed as minimalism or reductivism; Mouret's synthesis of the simple and the sensual is informed by a recognition of simplification as a means of expressing sensual purity. 'If I want to show the legs, I put more fabric on the body', he says. 'I am always looking for a mixture of skin and fabric.'

Mouret's pieces are characterized by high necklines and high hemlines, and by plunging décolletés matched by mid-length skirts. He seeks to create a daily wardrobe for women, introducing basics that look anything but. His 'tunic-top-dress' of 2009 is an apex of pragmatic elegance. His most famous design, however, was from his Autumn/Winter 2005–06 collection: the Galaxy, a plain, panelled, hourglass dress that made his name synonymous with pared-down glamour and sensuality, and drove his label into the realm of the A-list and the red carpet.

The Galaxy dress underscores the technical complexities that define Mouret as a true minimalist. It is a piece designed with the enhancement of the female form in mind, designed to use the body as the only decoration it needs; there is no further adornment. The integral structure holds the body in where it needs it and shows it off in the places where it does not. Mouret's attention to the female figure – and, importantly, the wearer's own attention to the female figure – marks him out among a new generation of advancing Purists. 'I'm not a minimalist,' he avers, 'because minimalism is to do with hiding the body, whereas I am working in the tradition of glamour and uniform.' But the notion of uniform in itself is inherently minimalist, and Mouret's clothes, inspired by the masculine tradition of workwear, are as much about making life easier for women as were those of McCardell and Karan. They have become the latter-day signifiers of the woman who has it all: a high-powered job that requires formal dressing, and an uproarious social life for which she wants to look alluring. No wonder his clothes are so popular in Hollywood costume departments; they speak volumes.

'When I started to get into draping,' Mouret recalls, 'I draped with flowers and decoration. And the women around me would say, "Take them off, we hate them!" It was always the women who were more straightforward than my vision of them. I design for the woman who enjoys being a woman.' Certainly this woman is a product of her time; the reason no one had yet designed with her

Less is ... Glamour

ROLAND MOURET

Autumn/Winter 2010–11 (opposite, left); Spring/Summer 2010 (opposite, right); Autumn/Winter 2009–10 (right): Bold colour and creative folding and drapery give Mouret's designs their verve; their strength comes from an overall vision of delicate but modern simplicity.

in mind was to do with the fact that women's social standing only really became stable and, to all intents and purposes, equal in the 1990s. Kors, Rodriguez and Mouret all encapsulated – and still encapsulate – a type of client who was effectively a newborn: a woman who had nothing to prove, and nothing to hide. Femininity was not a concept that needed tempering or starching any longer, so it naturally followed that the tenets and focus of minimalism also shifted.

'It was a reaction', says Mouret, 'to too much. What was before – we had bling and trophy girls – and now we don't have that. It's a woman in control of herself. If she has money, she doesn't like to show it.'

Notes
1 Lisa Armstrong, 'Fashion Talk: Catwalk Report '98', *Vogue* (UK), January 1998, pp. 102, 105.
2 Woody Hochschwender, 'Designers on a Quiet Road to Success', *New York Times*, 1 November 1988.
3 This and all other quotations from Michael Kors in this chapter are (unless otherwise stated) taken from an email from him to the author, May 2010.
4 Conversation with Michael Kors, November 2009.
5 Quoted in *Contemporary Fashion*, ed. Taryn Benbow-Pfalzgraf, Detroit (St James Press) 2002, p. 386.
6 This and all other quotations from Narciso Rodriguez in this chapter are taken from an email from him to the author, April 2010.
7 Lisa Armstrong, 'Cleaning Up', *Vogue* (UK), October 1996, p. 215.
8 Armstrong, 'Fashion Talk', p. 103.
9 This and all other quotations from Roland Mouret in this chapter are taken from a conversation between him and the author, June 2010.

Less is ... the Future

Technology, Construction and Historicism, 1998–2008

HUSSEIN CHALAYAN

Spring/Summer 2000: Chalayan's intellectual, scientific approach to womenswear brought a transformative and futuristic aspect to minimalism, one concerned not with the body's physicality but rather with what that body could achieve.

The physicality, tenderness and sensuality with which pretty minimalism treated the female form provided a mainstream expression for fashionable reduction, and it was easily understood, interpreted and imitated. But alongside the rise of glamour as part of the aesthetic, there was a striving for further purity and distillation of essence, one that came not from the athleticism of Michael Kors, the romanticism of Narciso Rodriguez nor even the utilitarian aspects of Roland Mouret. Other designers were searching for a means of sublimating femininity itself – not hiding or disguising its signifiers, as the Japanese designers had done in the 1980s, but minimizing minimalism itself. The aesthetic had been concerned with the female body and its dimensions and animation; its next move was towards sculpture and the creation of forms that did not in fact resemble clothing or anything humanoid.

It is noticeable that the ebb and flow of minimalism's popularity within fashion during its history have been linked very closely to the development and progression of the women's movement: Chanel and the liberation from the corset as women won the right to vote; American sportswear's role in the working lives of women; Pierre Cardin and the women's lib movement; the Japanese and the 1980s backlash against feminism; even, to some extent, Kors and Mouret with the newly liberated, financially independent breed of woman that emerged at the very end of the twentieth century. Minimalism had in general been a way of escaping gender stereotypes, whether by covering up or revealing the body in new ways and dimensions, making it plainer and creating a palette of sombre hues that meant the wearer could be taken seriously. In a reaction to the prettifying of the aesthetic that came about in the late 1990s, there arose an attachment to androgyny. Overt and complex construction became a means of attaining a transformative culmination of minimalism, a sort of high-tech negation of both form and function. These pieces

were not the pragmatic, wearable basics that such designers as Claire McCardell and Donna Karan had aimed to introduce to the sartorial canon; they were conceptual sculptures, tests of minimalism's fashionable boundaries, expressions of the *nec plus ultra* of functional womenswear.

One of the first, and most important, proponents of this trend was British-Cypriot designer Hussein Chalayan (born 1970), whose intellectual rigour and technical wizardry were as influential as those of the 1960s designers. Chalayan is as visionary as Chanel in the difference he has made to pre-existing conceptions of clothing, and can be classed with Rei Kawakubo and Martin Margiela in his creation of unexpectedly elegant pieces with a certain purity of line, vision and concept, and also in his avant-garde integrity and single-mindedness. Although his catwalk shows often resemble installations, revealing a marked sense of theatrical *mise en scène*, Chalayan's clothes and commercial collections are eminently wearable, practical and modern in their downplayed sense of style.

One of Chalayan's most iconic collections is 'Afterwords', his Autumn/Winter 2000–01 offering, which saw four models approach a set of four chairs around a circular coffee table. One by one they removed the grey cotton coverings from the chairs and stepped into them, folding back panels, Velcroing them in place, zipping integral seams together and standing in a line, each now wearing a slightly different grey dress. As they stood, stage crew dismantled the four chairs into a suite of suitcases and briefcases, which were placed next to the models. A final model entered and removed the central leaf from the coffee table, before standing in the circular hole it left, and pulling the rest of the table – which rose in tiers – up to her waist, where it hooked on to a belt and could be worn as a skirt.

Inspired by the plight of Chalayan's own Turkish-Cypriot relatives, who had fled persecution during the ethnic cleansing wars

HUSSEIN CHALAYAN

Autumn/Winter 2000–01: The
ultimate synthesis of fashion
and function, Chalayan's
table/skirt and dresses made
from armchair coverings
were inspired by Cypriot
refugees who carried their
belongings on their backs.

HUSSEIN CHALAYAN

Spring/Summer 1998:
Tubular wool dresses (left)
with integrated sleeves
reduced clothes to what
was barely even a minimum,
and rendered them more
as second skins.

Skirt by Simone Rocha,
shirt by Hussein Chalayan
(opposite).

in the years after Cyprus became independent in 1960, the collection was based on the notion of refugees being able to carry their homes with them wherever they went, and at short notice. The practical imperatives are essentially congruent with minimalism, but the vision is new. Chalayan seeks to reduce clothing to its absolute function; if anything, he aims to give it a more relevant functionality, because it can also act as something else. This is in line with the ethics of deconstruction, a movement or trope that aimed to question the prevailing mores of paying over the odds for a garment that looked as though it was falling apart or had already been worn to death; here Chalayan takes a reductivist angle to question the necessities of fashion, the very fundamental aspects of its existence. The dresses created from the chair coverings are simple in their nature; the four women wearing them appear to be attired in some kind of uniform. Their simple and fresh elegance cannot be questioned, though; after all, these women do not look drab or dowdy. The collection included luxurious tailored coats structured with irreverent drapery and highlighted with white piping that looked almost like a pattern drawn on to a toile; dresses also came in vibrant and vivid colours, layered to expose ruffles beneath flaps and cut-out hems.

Chalayan's Autumn/Winter 1998–99 collection, 'Panoramic', featured dresses, sweaters, tops and coats made from wool looped vertically over the body, with holes cut for head and feet, arms swinging freely in the larger hole created by the edge of the fabric. It called to mind the traditionally Japanese method of working in the round, freeing up the body with new dimensionality; collars in the same collection also recalled the sculptural qualities of Cardin's tailoring, rising to frame the face and covering the chin. A final sequence of models wore wool bodysuits and had their faces covered with wooden helmets, some with etiolated crania swooping behind them in mimicry of the elliptical swoops of fabrics around the body. Again, all Chalayan's tailoring was practical and

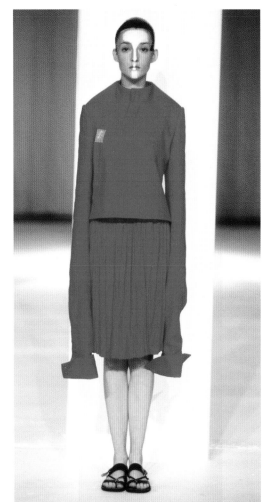

HUSSEIN CHALAYAN

Spring/Summer 1998 (right)
and 1999 (right, bottom):
Chalayan has re-evaluated
traditional womenswear
by playing with proportion
and expectations, giving his
work a distinctly modern,
even clinical feel.

wearable, finding elegance in the mid-length pleated skirts and flat shoes in the same way that a Comme des Garçons or Yohji Yamamoto collection renews femininity not with high heels and sex appeal but with a plain and sober appreciation of shape. It is interesting to note that Chalayan also cites Jean Muir as an inspiration.

Chalayan also shares with Comme des Garçons, Yamamoto and Muir a propensity for rustic simplification in a traditional workwear mode, although the more commercial aspects of his collections often go unnoticed in the wake of his visionary showpieces. In the collection for Autumn/Winter 1999–2000, 'Echoform', he featured not only the iconic opening look of a white plastic dress, modelled by Audrey Marnay, with animatronic panels that unfolded, lifted and slid out at the touch of a remote button, but also sheer cotton smock tops, collarless cropped jackets and crinkled, draped sundresses – one of which, on being inflated, smoothed out and, in its A-line silhouette, became a formal cocktail gown. There were also cream A-line dresses that spoke of futuristic frothiness: a cutaway section at the rear hemline revealed several more layers of skirts, yet it was not these layers that gave the dress its volume, but the stiff outer shell of material. The previous season's 'Geotropics' (Spring/Summer 1999) had also featured these severely cut tailored separates, with collars becoming tectonic juttings from the front of garments, as opposed to vertical adornment at neck height. The soundtrack to the show was plainsong and the models wore medical steri-strips in their hair, emphasizing Chalayan's overtly modern take on asceticism: he is informed by the arcane and there are aspects of medievalism to his work, but all is underpinned by his decidedly clinical modes of expression.

Chalayan has always played with his wearer's – and his audience's - expectations. His 'One Hundred and Eleven' collection for Spring/ Summer 2007 consisted of sporty separates worn with jackets that had integral hats that morphed

HUSSEIN CHALAYAN

A sporty, modern anorak
is given an almost tailored
aspect by the severity
of its cut.

into hoods, followed by a series of dresses that transformed themselves into new shapes by means of a computerized system of motors in the linings that reeled in wires attached to hems, sleeves and fastenings. The self-altering dresses were supposed to represent sartorial changes throughout the twentieth century: the first went from a hobble skirt and bustle of 1906 to a free-formed, shorter flapper-style dress. The final dress, and the final look of the show, transformed into vapour, the white chiffon around the model rising into her flying-saucer-shaped hat and leaving her completely naked.

'The press picks up all the eccentricities and neglects 95 per cent of what he does', said academic Andrew Bolton in 2001. 'He reminds me of Pierre Cardin or Paco Rabanne in the Sixties, designers who created clothes based on the architectural idiom.'[1] Chalayan's avant-garde approaches and inspirations, which range from animatronics to the creation of an entire eighteenth-century narrative for his graduation collection in 1993, are at odds with the pieces one finds in shops. That is not necessarily, as Bolton suggests, the fault of the press; nor is it a sign of suspicious prioritizing on the part of Chalayan. But it does speak of the modern proselytization of minimalism. In his shows, Chalayan presents aphoristic, headline-grabbing scenarios that serve to underline his sartorial intentions. Customers then retain a piece of this initiative with the purchase of a plain coat or some other eminently wearable garment. Chalayan's conceptual approach to the aesthetic is, in this way, as pragmatic as that of Karan or Miuccia Prada; it is the ideas intrinsic to his pieces that make them singular.

HUSSEIN CHALAYAN

The practical femininity of
Chalayan's clothes is often
pitted against a geometric,
scientific asceticism; hence, a
mannish blazer can become
an oversized women's coat
or a cutaway panelled dress.

High-tech Gothic: Bruno Pieters, Raf Simons and Gareth Pugh

Hard-edged and scientific though Chalayan's
pieces may be, they also retain an ethereal
quality, thanks to the designer's soft palettes and
his arcane and monastic treatment of cloth. This
fusion of sci-fi and sterile was present in much
minimalist fashion at the very beginning of the
twenty-first century, part of a retro-futuristic
aesthetic that seemed to convey cultural
confusion. We had, of course, reached the future
imagined for us by the likes of Cardin and André
Courrèges; but it was not comparable to those
iconic 1960s interpretations of it. Technological
advances came thick and fast, but general
existence was still recognizably twentieth
century in flavour. Designers began to address
this future–reality dichotomy in their collections,
creating pieces that were hyperbolically
intergalactic or extreme, but which owed much
to a historicist take on fashion and costume.

Minimalism once again became more gothic
in nature, not nostalgically – as it had been in the
hands of Ann Demeulemeester, for example – but
neo-gothic: notably dark, angular and slightly
oppressive in tone. Such designers as Bruno
Pieters, Raf Simons, Riccardo Tisci at Givenchy
and Gareth Pugh created a gothic vision with
the romance removed; it was clinical, scientific-
feeling, harsh and stark.

Pieters (born 1977) was yet another visionary
from the Royal Academy of Fine Arts in Antwerp
(as was Margiela, for whom he worked during his
early career). In Autumn/Winter 2001–02 Pieters
showed a couture collection of twelve suits that
showed an austerity of line similar to that of
McCardell but with the sumptuous elegance of
early Christian Dior. His tailoring did not borrow
from the masculine tradition at all, with box pleat
mid-length circle skirts and 1940s-style boxy
jackets topped off with sporty toggle fastenings;
his elision of past and present was obvious even
then. By Spring/Summer 2003, Pieters's style had

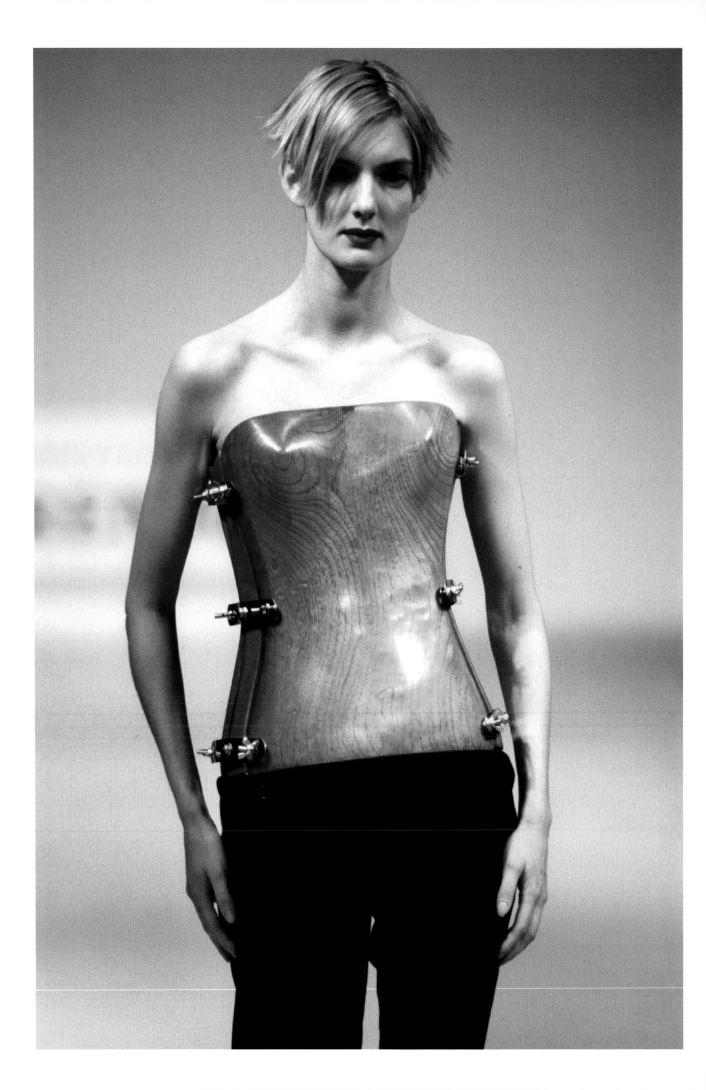

evolved into a darker vision of the feminine
sportswear purveyed by such designers as Kors;
his collection was rendered entirely in black
and white, with some adornment haphazardly
placed around shoulders and necklines. His
aesthetic bordered on grunge, mixing sleeveless
jersey sweatshirts with pleated skirts and long-
line leather coats, working in dark hues for
winter and in white, cream and putty for spring.

By Autumn/Winter 2004–05 Pieters's
designs had softened and lost their rock 'n' roll
edge, taking on a more monastic feel. Luxurious
boiled-wool princess coats showed a complexity
of cut and pattern that placed structure at the
heart of his aesthetic. His garments also made
much use of panelling, a technique essential
to the early American sportswear designers
because of the exigencies of mass production
at the time, but which Pieters used to create an
industrialized look that stood out among the
sleeker contemporary styles on the catwalk.
Where Rodriguez, Kors and Mouret favoured a
stylized hiding of construction, the next wave of
minimalists found it crucial to the externals of
a garment. Again, this element of conspicuous
construction – as seen in Chalayan's
groundbreaking shows and installations –
gave an impression of sci-fi sculpturalism
and intentional complexity to pieces that
were otherwise understated and sombre.

This hyperbolic understatement is
characteristic of the futuristic minimalism of
the time: Chalayan's clothes, as we have seen,
were complex beyond any surface scrutiny, but
he endeavoured to create in as plain a way as
possible. The feeling of the time was a self-
conscious paring down of aesthetic – not for
practicality's sake, but rather to show the
competency of design behind the clothes. This
foregrounding of design was a further attempt
to nullify existing notions of fashion, of dressing
and of minimalism itself.

Laird Borrelli wrote of Pieters's Autumn/
Winter 2005–06 collection: 'His best pieces had

Less is ... the Future

BRUNO PIETERS

Spring/Summer 2005 (right); Spring/Summer 2008 (right, bottom); Autumn/Winter 2009–10 (opposite): Pieters issues directives of modern minimalism with one eye on history, here referencing a pastoral seventeenth-century smocked shirt, Edwardian-style tailoring and an arcane, slightly gothic medievalist asceticism.

a timeless quality that evoked ... the century- and genre-skipping movie *Orlando*: light, feminine dresses, brocade coats, and pannier and bell skirts suggested everything from a modern-day Marie Antoinette to a contemporary Daisy Buchanan.'[2] Pieters's historical referencing comes in the form of garments that are intentionally similar in structure to recognizable pieces from the canon of historical costume, whether the smock shirts and jodhpurs of his Spring/Summer 2005 collection, summoning to mind seventeenth-century farm labourers and country gentlemen; the Victorian collars and leg o' mutton sleeves from Spring/Summer 2008; or the medieval cowls and gable hoods of Autumn/Winter 2009–10. Each of these references is fully worked into a scheme of modern clothing that is practical, wearable and thoroughly current. Pieters's methodology of minimalism, therefore, reduces the modern era into that out of which it was born. The minimizing of modernism should be anathema to minimalism as a form of design, given that it has been such a modernizing force within fashion, but Pieters's interpretation gives it relevance beyond the merely commercial.

Of course, the minimalism invoked by the Japanese in the early 1980s and by the Belgians later in that decade did not owe much to commerce, either, but it nevertheless represented a progression in aesthetic that was not at all backward-looking. The historicists of the 1990s and early 2000s were ironizing this perceived need for progress, turning on its head what was started by such designers as Cardin and Courrèges.

Raf Simons (born 1968) is another Belgian designer inspired by the past. His background is in industrial design rather than fashion, so the trend for structure and ergonomic clothing, such as that created by Chalayan and Pieters, represents a natural confluence of interests for him. Originally a menswear designer, Simons channels a retro-futurist style in his own-label collections, the most iconic of which was his Autumn/Winter 1999–2000 collection of plain

Less is ... the Future

RAF SIMONS

Simons's own-label collection is sober and plain, with modern accents, such as dropped shoulders, technofabrics and new silhouettes.

black capes, modern updates on ceremonial garb. Simons is an anti-fashion designer, shying away from movements, trends and mindsets and searching for the essence of individuality. He finds this in simple and historical clothes, inspired by youth movements, music culture and art.

In 2005 Simons became creative director at Jil Sander, after Sander left because of creative differences with the Prada group, which had bought the label in 1999. Simons brought to the label – which was already known for having been a catalyst in the simplifying of lines and the rise of popular purism in the 1990s – a sense, matching Sander's own, that clothes should not inhibit the woman who wears them, but should project her personality without projecting her sexuality. This is, of course, a traditional tenet of minimalism. After his Autumn/Winter 2010–11 show, Simons proclaimed that his audience consisted of 'women who have a target, and go for it'.[3]

'That unflinching Belgian pragmatism regarding the need for upper-echelon career clothes has ... become Raf Simons' brand-stabilizing trademark,' declared Sarah Mower after his Autumn/Winter 2007–08 collection, his third for Jil Sander, 'alongside the stamp of calm conceptualism he's bringing to the house.'[4] Simons's use of concept is not quite the same as that of Chalayan, who distils his concepts into the barrier-breaking parts of his shows in order that they be reflected on to his commercial pieces; Simons's concepts are woven well within the clothes, which are practical but never quotidian. The collection of 2007 in question featured monastic-style capes and lean suiting, minimalist tailoring that offered new focal points, and shift dresses.

Simons's collections for Jil Sander give traditional workwear a directional mode. For example, the tailored dresses he showed for Autumn/Winter 2008–09 were presented in sober grey wool and finished with architectural curlicues and swoops that added structure in unexpected places – the shoulder, the back seam, the hemline – all picked out with fluorescent linings.

That Simons is unafraid of colour represents yet another fusing of the various strands of minimalism so far discussed. He differs from the other minimalists of his ilk in his embracing of bright neons, even romantic pastels, rendered in everything from neoprene to chiffon and gauze, a predilection that underlines his sense of modernity in everyday existence. His designs recognize the commercial need for aesthetic pleasure; his work underscores the importance of this even when operating in the tradition of pared-down, minimalist tailoring.

The commercialization of minimalism, as we have seen, was inherent in the trend's progression throughout the twentieth century; by the twenty-first, such market appeal became less important to designers working within its constraints. The first decade of the century was yet another economic boomtime, which brought with it not only the accessibility associated with Kors and Rodriguez, and even Francisco Costa at Calvin Klein, but also the artistically skewed versions by Simons and the chance for experimentation within the genre, as seen in the hands of Chalayan. However, yet another graduate of London's Central Saint Martins college was to take minimalism to previously unscaled heights.

The work of Gareth Pugh (born 1981) is often described as 'wacky' or 'edgy', and doubtless these terms are fitting in certain contexts. Elements of the designer's back-catalogue cannot be described as minimalist in any way: the beaked clown suit of Autumn/Winter 2005–06; the bejewelled leather bodysuit of Spring/Summer 2006, adorned with bulbous, inflated 'growths'; and especially, perhaps, the inflatable velvet poodle suit from his Autumn/Winter 2006–07 collection. Yet Pugh's continued studies in volume, his attention to monochrome as key to his aesthetic, and the gothic undertones, medieval starkness and fascination with the arcane and the sinister that underpin his work are essentially qualities of a modern minimalist designer. And as Pugh's work has matured,

Less is ... the Future

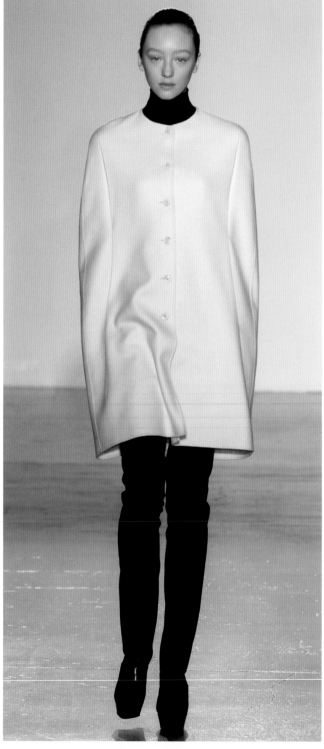

JIL SANDER

Autumn/Winter 2007–08
(opposite); Spring/Summer
2008 (below): Raf Simons's
designs for Jil Sander
combine a classic sense of
minimalist femininity with
a luxurious austerity; his use
of colour and volume adds a
prettiness that goes beyond
glamour and points to the
similar sartorial architecture
that Balenciaga pioneered.

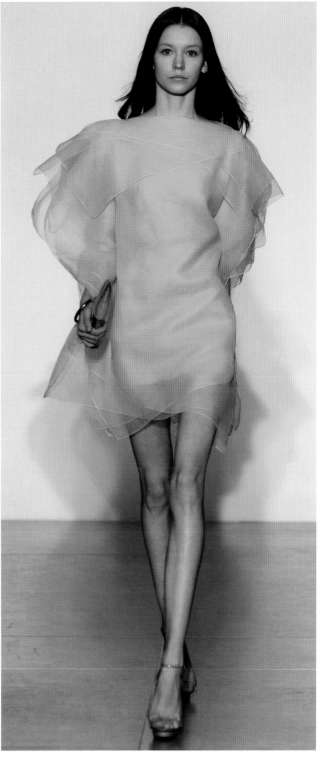

his dependency on and relevance to minimalism has become more pronounced.

Pugh's earliest collections focused on the interplay of black and white, whether in stripes or harlequin prints. These were scattered and stretched across vinyl, acetate and leather to create body-conscious, architectural pieces that explored corporeal dimensions in the same way that Miyake once did; that played with expectations and fashion mores just as Margiela had; that reinvented a version of femininity – or rather androgyny – that had as much of an impact as Kawakubo's. Pugh's deliberately sinister S&M aesthetic, his skewed proportions of vast shoulders and tiny corseted waists heralded a new silhouette, albeit not one that would be available on the high street without some re-evaluation. Pugh often takes his silhouette away from anything even vaguely humanoid, adding lumps and growths, just as Kawakubo did – although where her purpose was to disguise and ironize, Pugh's is to distort and question. For Spring/Summer 2007, Pugh created a black vinyl yoke that turned a model's arms into shiny black points, so that she resembled some kind of intergalactic spaceship or futuristic weapon more than she did a person.

Pugh also consistently covers his models' faces during shows, whether in clear plastic, so their features remain visible, with jaunty berets fashioned from binbags, or underneath Spring/Summer 2007's giant cuboid 'squarehead' hat. A distinct obscuring of physicality runs through Pugh's work; his models become futuristic goth-cyborgs in a further imagining of the endpoint of minimalism, when it minimizes to the extent that the wearer's existence is negated entirely.

But it was Pugh's Autumn/Winter 2008–09 collection that set him in a similar mode of structuralism and overt construction to those of Chalayan, Pieters and Simons. His rigid samurai-esque pieces fitted the brackets of both sci-fi futurism and medievalism, once again eliding the eras, presaging the timelessness with which

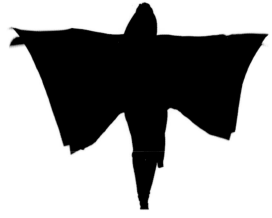

GARETH PUGH

Autumn/Winter 2009–10:
Pugh's stark but fluid
silhouettes (opposite) speak of
an aesthetic informed by the
arcane and the apocalyptic.

Autumn/Winter 2006–07
(below); Spring/Summer
2007 (below, right): Pugh is
concerned with historical
references and the end
point of geometry; his
fusion of the two creates
a distinctive modern
reductivism, retrospective
but also progressive.

Less is ... the Future

Jumpsuit by Louise Goldin,
leather chevron dress by
Gareth Pugh (opposite).

RICK OWENS

Owens's Californian vision
of gothic fashion (right) flits
between an apocalyptic
futurist aesthetic and sci-fi
purism, always pared back
and minimal but also
sculptural and inventive.

GARETH PUGH

Autumn/Winter 2010–11:
Chevron panelling and
geometric cuts reinforce
Pugh's darkly innovative
aesthetic, exploring body
dimensions and volume.

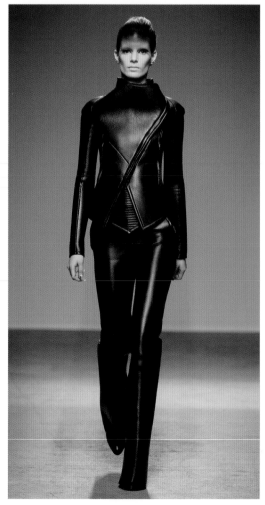

minimalism imbues clothing. When Pugh began showing his collections in Paris for Spring/ Summer 2009, he emphasized this concept with an entirely monochrome collection that featured Elizabethan ruffs alongside textured, tiled trenchcoats topped off with armour-like gauntlets. Even though some dresses were full-skirted and fluid, the theme of the show was structure, and one that encased rather than enveloped.

In 2006 consultant Michelle Lamy became financial backer to Pugh's label. Lamy's partner is designer Rick Owens (born 1962), whose own aesthetic draws on minimalism to create a grungy, apocalyptic vision of womenswear, one that has influenced some of Pugh's more recent work. Pugh's Autumn/Winter 2009–10 collection looked to history rather than the future, with sombre black and graphic cuts. 'This is not from a spaceship, it's from under the ground', Pugh said after the show, which included dresses, coats and kimono-style dresses belted with over-sized obis, all in black.[5] For Autumn/Winter 2010–11, Pugh worked in stiffened leather held together in chevron panels to create architectural suiting, coats and separates, again with no surface adornment but statement-like in their exploration of new bodily dimensions and volume.

Pugh's version of minimalism is one that flies in the face of its definition, and intentionally so. His collections repudiate what is wearable and what is appropriate, what is practical and pragmatic. It is only fitting, then, that his take on an enduring aesthetic should seek to place it so far beyond any recognizable point in time that even its being part of a movement is called into question. Nevertheless, Pugh's rigorous attention to simplicity of silhouette and form, regardless of his treatment of function, marks him out as the firebrand in a new wave of minimalism. His ingenuity inspired the next popular motion for the trend, for the time was ripe for a revival of minimalism.

Notes
1 Quoted in Caroline Roux, 'Catwalk to Istanbul', *The Guardian*, 29 September 2001, p. 40.
2 Laird Borrelli, 'Bruno Pieters', Style.com, 28 February 2005: style.com/fashionshows/review/F2005RTW-BPIETERS (accessed August 2010).
3 Quoted in Sarah Mower, 'Jil Sander', Style.com, 26 February 2010: style.com/fashionshows/review/F2010RTW-JLSANDER (accessed August 2010).
4 Sarah Mower, 'Jil Sander', Style.com, 20 February 2007: style.com/fashionshows/review/F2007RTW-JLSANDER (accessed August 2010).
5 Quoted in Tim Blanks, 'Gareth Pugh', Style.com, 4 March 2009: style.com/fashionshows/review/F2009RTW-PUGH (accessed August 2010).

Less is ... Now

The New Minimalist Revival, 2007–10

CÉLINE

Spring/Summer 2010:
Phoebe Philo's first collection
for the French house Céline
ushered in a new age of
sleek, modern minimalism,
a trend that took the fashion
world by storm.

As the first decade of the twenty-first century passed its halfway point, the seeds for a full-scale revival of minimalism in fashion had been sown just as surely as they had before the rise of Purism in the 1980s. Although it had continued as a tangentially fashionable aesthetic, reduction had not been at the forefront of tastes in the fashion industry or among the more general consuming public for more than a decade. The overall anti-fashion lifestyle that suited minimalism so well had, perhaps ironically, fallen out of fashion as tastemakers and trendsetters, influenced by the cult of celebrity and by music culture, veered into the mainstream. The zeitgeist became one of ostentatious display, which found its synecdoche (if not its pinnacle) in the release of Chanel's 'Forever' bag in December 2007. Made from alligator skin and with a clasp studded with more than 300 diamonds, it cost just over £100,000; a month later, Burberry released its 'Warrior' bag: alligator skin again, armour-plated and with a price of £13,000.

These 'It bags' have become a metaphor for the fashionable excess in the last months before the credit crunch: expensive, status-driven, ultimately expendable pieces that would be rendered obsolete the next season by a (potentially even more expensive) successor. It seems fitting to return to Paul Poiret's assertion, quoted earlier, that 'excess in matters of fashion is a sign of the end'.[1] The ultimate, and uncannily prescient, icon for this state of affairs was Damien Hirst's diamond-encrusted skull, unveiled in June 2007 and sold for £50 million in August. That summer it became increasingly obvious that the financial system as it was had become unstable, that a crash was unavoidable and that spending habits were about to change. There followed, of course, a certain amount of moralizing and fashion proselytizing, and the industry coined new phrases designed to encourage people to continue spending money: 'investment buy', 'price per wear' and 'recessionista' featured heavily in the reportage and fashion press of

the time. But neologisms aside, fashion needed a new identity that was more in step with public feeling. 'It may not feel like it at the moment,' wrote Clare Coulson in March 2007, 'but fashion is gradually becoming more pared down – a logical antidote to years of frills, flounces and feminine detailing. Well-designed, simple clothes will become increasingly relevant, just as they were when fashion last took a minimalist turn in the early 1990s.'[2]

Of course, designers and the show cycle often work up to sixteen months ahead of pieces that are actually in the shops, so, at the very beginning of the credit crunch, minimalism was a trend on the sidelines. But it was already a shaping force: the confluence of accessible, glamorous minimalism from the Americans with the hard-edged, directional style fostered in East London meant that popular taste had become attuned to simplicity of line and palette, and to a fashionable sense of austerity. For the Spring/Summer 2007 shows (and in the wake of a Spring 2005 collection from Martin Margiela), many designers had turned to the 1980s for inspiration, which meant – alongside neons, fluorescents and Lycra – a preponderance of sleek and unadorned body-conscious pieces and heavy structural detailing; the rise of the streamlined neo-goth look, meanwhile, ensured that colours were dark and sober, and silhouettes unfussy. 'Minimalism is more relevant than ever,' says Rob Phillips, creative director of the design school at London College of Fashion, 'and on so many levels: environmentally and stylishly. A non-definable outfit has more longevity than a seasonal trend. If you define yourself as a minimalist in the fashion sense, you could go through decades wearing the same thing, looking great. Though if we all did that, well – bang goes the whole fashion business.'[3]

This provides a glimpse at the logic behind the minimalist revival. It was driven by an artistic sense of the necessity and relevance of pruning back, becoming realistic once more, developing clothes that last as they are meant to and are not

Less is ... Now

The minimalist revival centres on clean lines and a reduction of detail, but is not restricted to tailoring or workwear; street style and casualwear have also become less fussy. Coat (foreground) by Stella McCartney, cream bib by Simone Rocha; leather trousers (background) by Gareth Pugh, jumper by Stella McCartney, shoes by Hussein Chalayan.

thrown away the next season. 'There is a new readiness to absorb zeitgeist tendencies, to transform and simplify them', says Jil Sander. 'I see a natural harmony between minimalism and the cyber-age. I feel a strong affinity to, say, the iPhone, a product which combines child-like amazement and curiosity with technical advancement to create an instant classic. Ends meet in everything that is truly graceful and elegant.'[4]

While the history of minimalism in fashion has always been intertwined with various social, political and cultural shifts, the early twenty-first-century popular revival of the aesthetic is more an economic movement than a social one. That consumers have less money to spend on clothing is obvious; that they wish to spend it on pieces that will not date quickly is logical. But where minimalism had previously held an allure for the iconoclasts and avant-garde of each generation, with the 2000s revival it became almost rehabilitated. It has not become part of mainstream culture – since it is still a means of producing challenging and intelligent clothing – but it has certainly come a long way from the age when it was a means of rebelling against fashion's status quo. Minimalism became a way of perpetuating sales in a bleak economic climate. Not only did consumers want and need durable, timeless pieces, but also they were under instructions from the style press to reform their shopping habits: to shun so-called 'fast fashion' and purchase pieces ethically, to be willing to spend a little more for a better-quality item that would last longer and cost less in terms of natural resources, waste and pollution.

Nevertheless, it took time for minimalism to re-establish a grip on the fashion consciousness. London design duo Justin Thornton and Thea Bregazzi, who work under the label Preen, provided one of the earliest indications of the direction fashion was taking. Their Autumn/Winter 2007–08 show melded a futuristic aesthetic with one that was inherently 1980s, and in so doing

created a look that would become a staple of new minimalism for several seasons to come. Stark but sensual, plain but pretty, low-octane but luxurious: body-conscious dresses with medieval-inspired cowls, hoods and bell sleeves; hot-pink tulip skirts rendered in neoprene with frilled hems that were structural rather than frothy; decoration by way of construction, with pin-tucks and horizontal pleating effects. Preen's design directives are also heavily indicative of the revivalist attitude to minimalism; they aim to create practical, timeless clothes that owe some of that timelessness to an intangible luxe quality.

'Fabrics have developed so that the look is smooth and minimal but the handle is soft and sumptuous', says Thornton. 'And most people prefer simplicity; women today don't want to look like they have tried too hard, they need to feel modern and directional, in control and still sexy.' Preen's collections embrace deconstruction, neo-goth, glamour, futurism and luxurious modern basics, all from a standpoint of overtly constructed minimalism that works to look both functional and fresh, modern and timeless. 'For us that is the challenge', says Bregazzi. 'Often the more simple a garment is to look at, the harder it is to make.'[5]

This is an important trope of modern minimalism, where the emphasis lies on hard-won quality and durability. For Autumn/Winter 2008–09, many designers were galvanized into minimalism by the perceived need for long-lasting and classic pieces, with the style press heralding 'The New Austerity', and the likes of Prada, Louis Vuitton and Yves Saint Laurent all showing subdued and pared-down collections. Prada, although not strictly minimalist, focused on 1940s-style midi-length dresses in thick, heavy black lace and silk; necklines were high and hems were low. For Louis Vuitton, Marc Jacobs (born 1963) created peg trousers and circle skirts, camel coats with concealed fastenings, and classic blouses and polo necks from sumptuous wools but in a palette of washed stones, creams and neutrals. Stefano Pilati (born 1965) at Yves Saint

PREEN

Autumn/Winter 2007–08 (opposite); Autumn/Winter 2009–10 (right); Spring/Summer 2010 (far right); Pre-Fall 2010 (right, bottom); Autumn/Winter 2010–11 (far right, bottom): Preen's body-conscious aesthetic brought back an awareness of shape and colour. Its bandage dresses, cutaway pieces and fluid styles heralded a new consciousness in the collections.

Less is ... Now

Autumn 2008 saw a season of luxurious minimalism on the catwalks, with three of the most influential labels choosing to show sumptuously elegant but heavily understated collections: Louis Vuitton (opposite, left); Prada (opposite, right); and Yves Saint Laurent (right).

Laurent showed his collection on a flock of models styled in identikit black pudding-bowl wigs with black lipstick. This austere army of automatons was dressed in re-imagined tailoring: carrot trousers, bagged out at the hips and narrowed at the ankles; wool blazers panelled with silk or cropped as cocoon-style boleros; no visible fastenings and few accessories.

These collections marked the re-emergence of minimalism as a key trend and a mainstream mode of fashion; they also gave the aesthetic new verve and edge, as well as new socio-economic relevance. The piety that had come with minimalism in the 1980s – that is, an opting out of mainstream fashion and its brasher qualities – now came with an opting *in* to some of the new environmental and ethical concerns informing mainstream fashion. Minimalism was a responsible way of consuming: fashion with a social conscience. 'The new mood in fashion is serious', explained *Vogue* in 2008. 'Serious about cloth, cut, quality, women, style, and very serious about wealth and how to express personal fortune and privilege in juddery economic times.'[6] The image of minimalism had also shifted slightly; its hyperbolic new starkness was intentionally challenging after a decade of frivolity and 'bling', hence Pilati's bewigged army, which has become an iconic image in the fashion archive, marching for change. 'The "stealth wealth" of the Nineties did not necessarily express an intellectual or intelligent angle – now it does', said trend-forecaster Martin Raymond. 'A generation of fortysomethings, who grew up through the designer decade – call them Scuppies (socially conscious, upwardly mobile) – are defining themselves through a sense of austerity ... Instead of grazing and gorging, we want to invest in better and less.'[7] This ideology is the reason minimalism continues to be the defining trend into the 2010s, whether designers have adopted it in the guise of tailoring, elegant eveningwear, sportswear or the gothic. It is an aesthetic that pervades the current fashion consciousness.

Mainstream Minimalism

The new fashion in turn has also been reflected on the high street, not only by the wholesale introduction of pieces that, even three years earlier, would have classified as difficult sellers, but also with the appearance of minimalist-minded brands, identifying themselves specifically as retailers of discreet, high-quality design. Swedish brand COS, or Collection of Style (an offshoot of the H&M empire), is known for a pared-down, luxurious aesthetic priced somewhere between designer lines and high-street offerings, and its launch in March 2007, in London, could not have been better timed to cater to the nascent popular taste for reductivist clothing. Grey cocoon coats with rounded, dropped shoulders and inconspicuous grosgrain trim; bucket pockets attached to the exterior of cotton shift dresses and apron skirts; merino jumpers with exposed zips at the back: these everyday, functional basics and separates are, in some ways, a return to what such designers as Claire McCardell had attempted to create. Yet the technology of mass production is now sophisticated enough to deliver her vision. Reduction is no longer a matter of function, but a deliberate aesthetic choice. 'In a fashion scene dominated by instantly recognizable designer looks, or instantly recognizable celebrity designer looks, or lairy and press-generating statement pieces, COS is anonymously, whisperingly cool', wrote Polly Vernon at the time. 'It's muted and chic, a bit Jil Sander, a bit Helmut Lang.'[8] Such explicit comparison to designers of this ilk underscores COS's determinedly minimalist brand identity; and that so-called 'challenging' pieces should be available on the high street and, more importantly, should sell – and in such numbers – underlines the fashion landscape of the time and the place of minimalism at its very heart.

For Autumn/Winter 2009–10, Japanese high-street chain Uniqlo announced a collaborative capsule range designed by none other than Jil Sander. '+J' for Uniqlo was the zenith of the modern minimalist revival, in terms of awareness and acceptance beyond the realms of the fashion industry and the relatively short reach of the catwalks. The store, known for its casual basics and streetwear, is a success story of essential garments, well made and fairly priced; the addition of Sander – whose name is synonymous with minimalism, the rise of Purism and the pared-down look representative of a whole decade – is a clear stamp of approval and intention from those on both sides of the cash registers.

'When I decided to join Uniqlo, I deliberately opted for a basics company', explains Sander. 'Producing quality for the mass market seems more visionary to me now, as fashion is one of the most important languages of globalism. The purism that I advocate highlights the individual without stressing local and ethnic differences; it invites everyone into the twenty-first century. It is my dream that the +J collection will win partisan status one day and turn into something like a club.' Her seasonal offerings have certainly been well received. Structured blazers, tailored with femininity in mind but borrowing from the masculine tradition, and sharp shirts mix with more urban pieces, such as a puffa jacket and a trench coat, while there are casual classics and basics on offer too: slub T-shirts and knits, cigarette pants and men's suiting. All are immaculately cut and perfectly unadorned. Suzy Menkes wrote that the collection had perhaps 'sparked a revolution', while Calgary Avansino of British *Vogue* described the collaboration as 'an act of genius'.[9]

Clothes for Modern Living

The economic importance of New Minimalism cannot be overemphasized, and represents an interesting divergence from the aesthetic's previous social function, that of championing and furthering the role of women at crucial points in

COS

Autumn/Winter 2010–11:
Swedish label COS
(Collection of Style) has
brought streamlined
modern minimalism
to the high street.

the history of liberation and equal opportunities. But the revival has had an impact on the contemporary sense of femininity. The credit crunch of 2008 was billed at the outset as a 'women's recession' (one that would result in a large number of female redundancies), introducing a gendered type of paranoia to the workplace, as there had been in the 1950s and again in the 1980s. The responses at these points had been, respectively, the monastic styles of American sportswear and the advent of Purism in the face of Lacroix's High Femininity aesthetic. Once again, working women were in need of a modern working persona and a wardrobe to match, and collections from such designers as Stella McCartney, Phoebe Philo at Céline (a label formerly designed by Michael Kors) and Hannah MacGibbon at Chloé gave them just that.

The Spring/Summer 2010 collection by Philo (born 1973) for Céline was era-defining in its minimalist take on clean and fresh feminine clothing: toffee-coloured leather T-shirts and skirts worn with camel capes and nude bodysuits ushered in a plainness of line that was striking in its combination of high-mindedness and luxury. The following season, Philo once again showed clothes of the most luxuriously utilitarian nature. They seemed to sum up, on the back of a more general move towards minimalism in fashion but also independently, what it really meant to be creating fashion at the time. 'Phoebe refers to her luxuriously utilitarian collection as "a wardrobe, an ABC of clothes"', wrote Penny Martin. '[This sounds] less like a prescription for modern dressing and more a formula for modern living.'[10] Philo's pieces are determinedly pragmatic and wearable – and therefore commercial – but also highly intelligent and aspirational; they represent the modern incarnation of minimalism, which wears both its intellectual and commercial credentials with equal balance. It was the logical next step after the New Austerity of Autumn/Winter 2008–09, and, where Uniqlo and COS had brought the aesthetic to a wider audience, Philo

Less is ... Now

STELLA MCCARTNEY

Autumn/Winter 2010–11:
McCartney is another of
the three young, female,
British designers to turn
to minimalism for the
twenty-first century. Her
feminine tailored separates
speak to the needs of the
modern woman.

reasserted its roots in high fashion and its intrinsic link to the fortunes and fate of modern femininity.

Likewise, the Autumn/Winter 2010–11 collection by McCartney (born 1971) summed up professional tailoring for working women, with elegant wool trouser suits and coats in felt and wool, decorated only by a notched lapel here, the incision of a pocket there. MacGibbon (born 1972) created for Chloé nostalgic and elegant tailored pieces in a neutral palette of nudes and beige. Sarah Mower noted 'an early-Armani-like jacket that might have jumped out of *Vogue*'s pages in the post-women's lib era – when dashing to work while looking enthusiastically businesslike was the thing'.[11]

Another noteworthy difference in the modern revival of minimalism is that it is not confined to workwear, but pervades all genres of clothing, from sportswear to eveningwear. Glamorous minimalist eveningwear, of the sort designed by Kors and Narciso Rodriguez, is nothing new, but the modern version is both softened and more stark, less overtly sexy, relying more on length and drapery and with a narrower use of colour. Francisco Costa (born 1961) has taken Calvin Klein in a lighter, more feminine direction since he became senior designer in 2003, and, although his designs for daywear work in a similar vein to those of Preen – a sculpted but fluid silhouette, slightly clinical in its futuristic cleanliness – his visions for after dark are more organic, with floor-length shift dresses and long-sleeved, narrow-line maxidresses that sweep the floor. There is a sense with his pieces for evening that Costa is working to the traditionally minimalist mindset of designing through the fabric rather than with it; there is something rather a priori about his full-length dresses.

This is also true of Colombian-born designer Haider Ackermann (born 1971), another minimalist who studied at the Royal Academy of Fine Arts in Antwerp, and whose sinuous, sweeping dresses have become a quiet institution worn on red carpets only by those in the know during the late 2000s. His pieces mix high and low culture,

Less is ... Now

CHLOÉ

Autumn/Winter 2010–11:
Hannah MacGibbon's
tailoring at Chloé is
masculine in cut but
feminine in inspiration.

creating elegance and formality with the techniques and inspirations of streetwear: a Madeleine Vionnet-esque floor-length silk dress is worn with an obi-belted leather gilet, or a circle-cut geometric cocoon coat, reminiscent of Poiret, with leather leggings. 'Haider Ackermann has a forward-thinking view of clothes in which women can participate by unzipping a peplum from a leather jacket, choosing how to place a flowing collar or how far to open the zipper on an ankle-length skirt', declared Menkes of his Autumn/Winter 2010–11 collection.[12] Fluidity of form as well as styling makes for a functional expression of modern elegance. It is an unexpected by-product of clothes that are often tight-fitting, highly structural and unashamedly luxe, but his use of light and draped materials, such as silk and leather, are proof of his philosophy of working according to the physical needs and expressions of the body and the female form.

For his Spring/Summer 2010 collection, Ackermann experimented not only with the draping and layering of silks, leather and gauze, but also with knotting, in a purist gambit that creates garments that emanate from a single focus. 'I wanted everything to start from one point', he told *Ten* magazine. 'The neck – always at the neck. It's aristocratic.'[13] Ackermann's pieces are all deeply sensual and feminine, with long skirts often cut away at the front or deeply slit, and leather treated and washed several times to give a softness similar to that of a human hide, but they are reserved and ascetic in their sensuality; nothing is revealed by an Ackermann skirt or top. According to Armand Limnander, of the *New York Times*, his clothes 'convey a strong, sexual charge that never [feels] forced or vulgar', with all the sense of physicality countered by cowled hoods and yokes that feel sporty as well as arcane and ascetic.[14]

Sportswear is, of course, a long-standing development ground for minimalism, although the American sportswear of McCardell and Mildred Orrick is a far cry from the more literal meaning of

Less is ... Now

HAIDER ACKERMANN

Autumn/Winter 2007–08 (right, top and bottom); Spring/Summer 2008 (opposite): Ackermann's medieval aesthetic is paired with a simple elegance that updates even the most classic of monastic shapes.

the term. Their shirtwaisters and jersey dresses were sporty when compared to the more formal mode of dress in the 1930s and 1940s, but little of what they created was actually for playing a sport in. New York designer Alexander Wang (born 1984) has no intention of his pieces being worn for sport either, but they do rely on a sect of minimalism that references athleticism and activity in its appearance. 'My aesthetic has always been centred on something clean and pure in its perspective', he says. 'For me the most important thing is to create a strong point of view that people want to wear and experience.'[15] Springing from a new-wave grunge culture in the late 2000s, Wang become known for defining and distilling that holy grail for fashion editors: off-duty model style. Indeed, in this way he is not dissimilar to such designers as Ann Demeulemeester, whose aesthetic paid tribute to the nonchalance of the very women modelling her collections.

Wang's early collections of denim and jersey basics were the epitome of well-styled, functional dressing. His later collections moved him into the realms of American sportswear proper, when he began to create garments with a complexity belied by their jersey components: marl-grey jumper dresses for Spring/Summer 2010 with tan-leather panelling and dolman sleeves, for example, referenced at once an American football kit and a cocktail dress. In the same collection, Wang riffed on the heritage of garments, turning trench coats into minidresses with fishtail skirts, and giving formal chinos a second, elasticated waist so they resembled jogging bottoms. The concept behind Wang's clothes is streetwise wearability and a simplicity born of function and context. His Autumn/Winter 2010–11 collection saw a similar ironizing of the pinstripe suit, deconstructed into coat dresses and cutaway negligee-style shifts. There were camel capes, too, and draped jersey dresses: references to the originators of the genre.

American sportswear was thus a prefiguring of the state of fashion now, driven by an overwhelming popular interest in a form of

HAIDER ACKERMANN

Autumn/Winter 2009–10 (opposite); Spring/Summer 2010 (right); Autumn/Winter 2008–09 (far right): Fluid, sinous shapes in satin, silk and fine leather are hallmarks of Ackermann's minimalism, rendered in drapery and ruching.

ALEXANDER WANG
Spring/Summer 2010
(opposite); Spring/Summer
2008 (right); Autumn/Winter
2010–11 (right, bottom):
Wang has reinvented
minimalism according to the
modern rules of American
sportswear, using materials
such as jersey and denim,
and streetwear as a
template, as well as
introducing notions of
deconstruction.

design that suited a moment historically, socially and economically. Minimalism by its very definition is not a trend to fall completely out of favour with the industry at any point, since its protean quality is the root of its sustainability. And it seems to be informing many contemporary young designers, such as Swedish label Nakkna, which creates simple, everyday jersey and cotton pieces – many of them unisex – according to a pared-down sensibility that mixes pragmatism with concept and is proof that minimalist design is not something too highbrow to live in. Paris-based designers Kaito Hori (born 1977) and Iku Furudate (born 1976) are the names behind the label Commuun, and produce collections of geometrically panelled suiting and shift dresses made exclusively from natural and organic fabrics. They believe that minimalism is the ideal vehicle for a more considerate type of fashion: 'People want to be pure and honest again.'[16] Meanwhile, many accessories designers, such as Florian Denicourt (born 1977), are also working within a minimalist remit. 'I am working with very classic forms,' he says, 'and I am inspired humanly and architecturally.'[17]

It speaks of its fashionability and adaptability that minimalism is the mode in which popstar-turned-designer Victoria Beckham (born 1974) has chosen to work, and her sharp but feminine pieces draw on the pretty, pared-down workwear aesthetic of the early 2000s.

Finnish designer Heikki Salonen (born 1979) showed his Autumn/Winter 2010–11 collection of stylishly severe tailoring as part of London's Fashion East initiative. Salonen claims: 'The attitude of our clothes is no-nonsense. They fulfil their destiny when they are worn – we are creating clothes for everyday fashion moments. For designers, it's more rewarding to make their mark with their own handwriting, rather than just being trendy.'[18] Salonen's sophisticated but streetwise pieces have a traditional but retro edge that links them directly to the purist tailoring of the 1990s, and are similarly complex in the way in which

Less is ... Now

COMMUUN

Autumn/Winter 2010–11:
Commuun (right) sees
minimalism as a vehicle for
ethical change, using natural
and organic materials.

FLORIAN DENICOURT

Accessories designer
Denicourt (right, bottom)
extends the tenets of
minimalism to high-quality
leather goods.

NAKKNA

Autumn/Winter 2010–11:
Swedish label Nakkna
creates fluid, unrestrictive
and often unisex pieces
(opposite) in jersey and
simple cotton, inspired
by the grunge minimalism
that is currently so popular
in Europe.

VICTORIA BECKHAM

Autumn/Winter 2010–11:
Even the collections by
popstar-turned-designer
Victoria Beckham (right, top
and bottom) owe much to
the revival of minimalism,
with glamorous gowns in
simple, flowing shapes.

HEIKKI SALONEN

Autumn/Winter 2010–11:
Finnish designer Heikki
Salonen is inspired by the
1990s grunge movement
and creates tailored
separates in a downbeat and
androgynous vein (opposite).

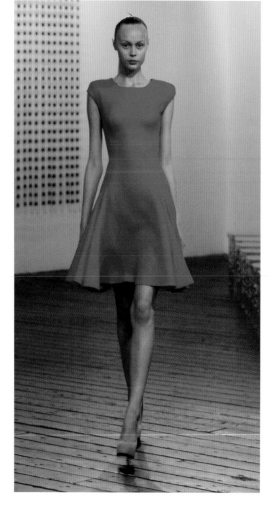

they combine masculine influences with
pragmatic design solutions for the everyday
feminine existence. They are minimalist in notion,
if not in construction. 'It's like defining the
garments almost to the level of a symbol', he
says, 'so they start living their own life.'

We have not heard the last of minimalism;
rather, it has become an emblem in modern
fashion. It not only represents a heritage of strong
design, innovation, intellectualism and a wealth
of fashion history, but is also heavily accented by
the human development of fashion and dress, in
that it is primarily an aesthetic that meant that
women could live their own lives, too.

Notes

1 Paul Poiret, *My First Fifty Years*, London (Gollancz) 1931,
   p. 289.
2 Clare Coulson, 'A Classic Case of the Basics', *Daily
   Telegraph* online, 14 March 2007: telegraph.co.uk/fashion/
   shoppingandfashion/3359570/a-classic-case-of-the-
   basics.html (accessed August 2010).
3 Email from Rob Phillips, September 2009.
4 This and all other quotations from Jil Sander in this
   chapter are taken from an email from her to the author,
   May 2010.
5 Email from Justin Thornton and Thea Bregazzi, May 2010.
6 Harriet Quick, 'The New Austere', *Vogue* (UK), September
   2008, p. 92.
7 Quoted in *ibid*.
8 Polly Vernon, 'COS – It's Worth It', *Observer Woman*,
   4 November 2007, p. 24.
9 Suzy Menkes, 'Jil Sander Bathes in the Glow of Uniqlo',
   New York Times, 6 June 2010; Calgary Avansino quoted
   in Carola Long, 'Plain and Simple: The Uniqlo Formula',
   The Independent, 25 June 2009.
10 Penny Martin, 'Phoebe Philo Designs the Clothes Women
   Actually Want to Wear', *The Gentlewoman* 1 (Spring/
   Summer 2010), p. 51.
11 Sarah Mower, 'Chloé', style.com, 9 March 2010: style.com/
   fashionshows/review/F2010RTW-CHLOE (accessed
   August 2010).
12 Suzy Menkes, 'Chic Severity with Head Held High',
   International Herald Tribune, 8 March 2010.
13 Quoted in 'Haider Ackermann: Technique and Draping',
   Ten (Spring/Summer 2010), p. 67.
14 Armand Limnander, 'Moment: Haider Ackermann',
   New York Times, 5 October 2009.
15 Email from Alexander Wang, June 2010.
16 Email from Commuun, April 2010.
17 Email from Florian Denicourt, May 2010.
18 Email from Heikki Salonen, June 2010.

Picture Credits

Index

First published 2011 by

Merrell Publishers Limited
81 Southwark Street
London SE1 0HX

merrellpublishers.com

British Library Cataloguing-in-Publication data:
Walker, Harriet.
Less is more : minimalism in fashion.
1. Fashion design – History – 20th century.
2. Minimal design – History – 20th century.
I. Title
746.9'2'0904-dc22

ISBN 978-1-8589-4544-6

Produced by Merrell Publishers Limited
Designed by Nicola Bailey
Project-managed by Rosanna Lewis
Indexed by Vanessa Bird

Printed and bound in Hong Kong

HARRIET WALKER writes on fashion for *The Independent* newspaper and AnOthermag.com. She has also contributed to *AnOther Magazine*, SHOWstudio.com, Dazed Digital and *W*, *Wonderland* and *Glamour* magazines.

AUTHOR'S ACKNOWLEDGEMENTS

Thanks to: Archie Bland for his kindness, patience and love; my mum and dad for their endlessly helpful suggestions; my wonderful sisters, Cathy and Sophie, for their faith and pride; Susannah Frankel for her wisdom, advice and encouragement; Lisa Markwell for commissioning the article from which this grew; Agata Belcen and Atlanta Rascher for their beautiful images; Carola Long, Gemma Hayward and Lee Holmes for their support; Elizabeth Byng for her knowledge and time; Emma, Rachel, Claire, Alma and Vince for clinking glasses with me at the beginning and end of this process; Iain R. Webb, Penny Martin and Rob Phillips; Rosemary Harden and Elaine Uttley at the Bath Fashion Museum; Louisa Collins at the V&A; Kaat Debo at the Modemuseum Antwerp; all the designers involved and everyone at Merrell; and Condé Nast for the use of its archives.

Front cover: Matthew Ames (p. 13)

Back cover, clockwise from top left: Donna Karan (pp. 84–85); André Courrèges (p. 61); Bruno Pieters (p. 151); Hussein Chalayan (p. 140)

Page 2: Preen, Autumn/Winter 2007–08

Pages 6–7: Yves Saint Laurent, Autumn/Winter 2008–09

Page 192: Phoebe Philo's collections for Céline encapsulate the clean luxury of the modern minimalist revival.

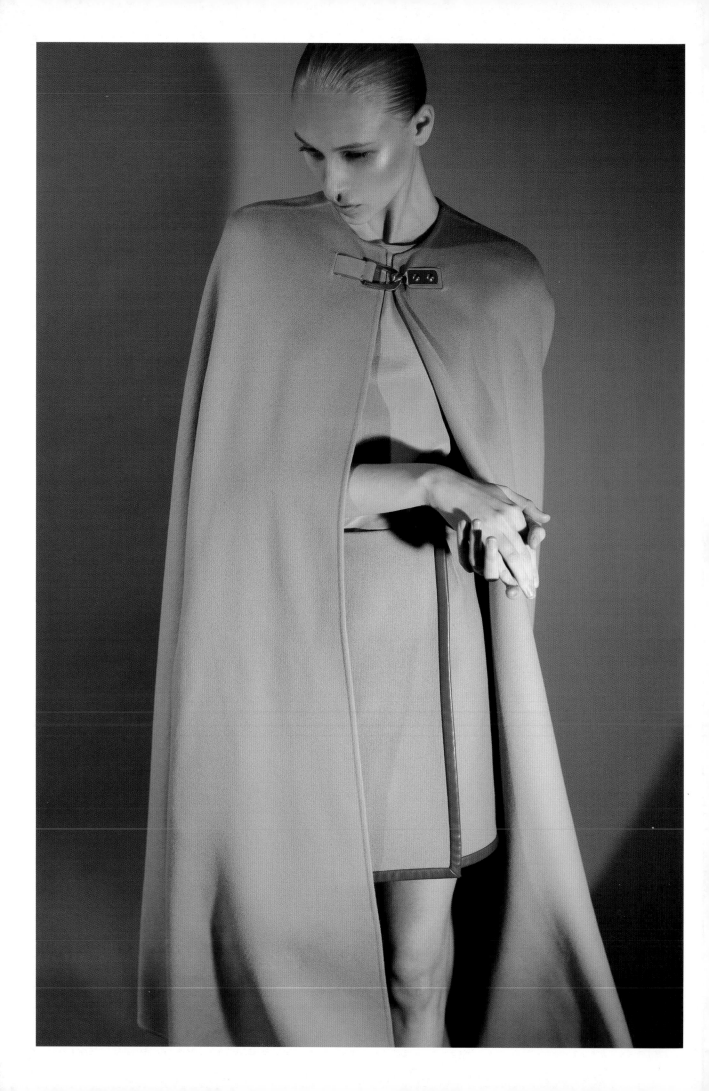